UNCHAINED

UNCHAINED

A Journey to the Soul
from Head to Heart

TONYA WHITTLE

NEW YORK

LONDON • NASHVILLE • MELBOURNE • VANCOUVER

UNCHAINED
A Journey to the Soul from Head to Heart

Published in New York, New York, by Morgan James Publishing. Morgan James is a trademark of Morgan James, LLC. www.MorganJamesPublishing.com

ISBN 978-1-64279-556-1 paperback
ISBN 978-1-64279-557-8 eBook
Library of Congress Control Number: 2019938264

Copywriters:
Christine Gordon
Manly Mann Media

Cover Design by:
Rachel Lopez
www.r2cdesign.com

Interior Design by:
Bonnie Bushman
The Whole Caboodle Graphic Design

Morgan James is a proud partner of Habitat for Humanity Peninsula and Greater Williamsburg. Partners in building since 2006.

Get involved today! Visit
www.MorganJamesBuilds.com

Dedicated to all the Wild Soul Women who have been chained, broken down, conditioned to be something you are not. As you unchain yourself and rise, may you take the world with you.

Personal Dedications:

To all those on my journey who helped me down, for you led me on the journey, and I would be remiss to not give you credit for the most amazing journey of my life.

To those who stood with me, by me, or led me—especially Regina Wright—my thanks is merely not enough. My soul is wild and free and you have been a huge part of that.

To my dogs—Tetley & Lexie Lou—for you have taught me what wild really is. You have shown me when to rest and when to go. My life is complete with you in it.

To my husband, for brave is the man who loves a wild woman.

Special Dedications: Rebecca Parsons, Tracy Allen, Jamie Lynn McCabe for supporting and making this book possible.

TABLE OF CONTENTS

PROLOGUE

There would be no life without woman. Momma Gaia, Mother earth and every woman who has born life through her is the very essence of humanity. It could not exist without the divine and sacred feminine that can create and give birth to life, our very existence indebted to the feminine.

And how has she been repaid? We have been hunted, raped, burned, suffocated and stuffed into a box for fear of our lives.

Trauma studies show that trauma changes our DNA. Holocaust survivor's grandchildren are showing less resilience to trauma than previous generations even though they did not experience it. It is coded in our DNA. Our ancestors literally pass on their trauma and studies on epigenetics and a host of studies from Harvard, The University of British Columbia, and others are proving what ancient wisdom and the wise old ones have been saying for centuries. The advancements in the last 5 years are stunning in showcasing how trauma changes us.

Learned fear of trauma is also a very real aspect. People who experience major trauma often pass on their own fears, their own coping mechanisms and behaviors. Residual and learned trauma can and do influence our world, our lives and how we live it.

Wouldn't it be fair to say that our mothers and grandmothers trauma is passed down to us, then? That even if we didn't experience it we can still hold the fear of it, the awareness of it, the knowledge of it in our cells?

Wouldn't the witch-hunt, the abuse, the rape, the violence that women have endured be alive in our cells today and impacting our own resilience to it? Couple that with our own experiences of abuse, trauma, being second all the time—wouldn't that impact our decisions, our lives, who we become because all of this stuff is stuck inside of us that we don't understand and don't have permission to explore?

Many faiths around the world believe that our ancestors are still with us, inside of us, that what they experience became also our experiences and when we healed, we not only healed ourselves but we healed them. And in the modern Western society, trauma studies and MRIs are showing what the wise ones knew for centuries but were burned at the stake for practicing.

Our cells remember the things our parents, grandparents have experienced. Our beliefs, our fears, our conditioning is not only ours but ancestors for generations back.

We carry it all. And then we carry our own. And we're not prepared for life, we don't cope, we are in a changing world and we don't know how to process our emotions or experiences because we live in a world that teaches us to hide what we feel, to pretend, to make better, to look away, to wear a mask. So, we stuff it all down, we pretend, we get by, we waste away, soulless, disconnected.

It all turns toxic inside of us, turning our lives malignant, changing us, controlling us, living in the space of never being able to get a full breath, drowning while on dry land, desperately searching and seeking for something, not realizing it's the need to live, to feel, to be fully alive, that we're so desperately searching for.

Women have been put down, beaten down, kept in line with fear of their safety for generations. But there was a time when the wild woman ruled the earth, when the goddess was revered, when the heartbeat of the earth was sacred and humble. When divine masculine rose to meet her in her space through love, elevation, passion and connection to all that is.

We are being called to bring this back. Not to smash men, not to smash true divine masculine but to smash the patriarchy that makes men's purpose, dreams and lives more important than women's. To smash the paradigm that thrives and breeds on fear. To smash the paradigm that allows rape, rape culture and the abuse of women, children, animals and the planet.

We are being called to smash the belief systems that cause us to half live, live in fear, and be disconnected from all that is. The world is in crisis and MORE STUFF won't fix it, more numbing and pretending and another mask and another layer won't change it.

What will change it is a return to our wild home, our own wild soul.

Sometimes things get messy, and we find comfort in things that aren't necessarily good. We find comfort and solace in food or in the arms of strangers. We develop habits, patterns and coping skills because we are all trying to find a way to survive this life—to fit in, to belong, to feel good, to feel like we matter and that our lives are important.

We get messed up because we see and feel one thing but we're conditioned so we forget it, we lose part of ourselves in the conforming. In fact, in order to conform we *must* lose part of ourselves. We cannot conform and remain in our truth. We must give up that truth in order to survive a life where who we are must be contained.

Our spark is doused. Our wild is tamed. Our hopes stomped on. Our hearts ripped out. They say they're just preparing us for the real world. They told us we could be anything until we're a certain age, then we must grow up and get real jobs, give up the fantasy, the believing, the hoping and dreaming.

We shrivel up and die a little more inside. We "get through" our days staying stuck in jobs, relationships, places we aren't happy because we think we are supposed to have it all together. We die a little more inside each day. We exist. We barely live. We learn to look outside of ourselves for happiness, approval, acceptance and we put ourselves last. We fill everyone else's tank and we run on fumes for as long as possible. When the fumes run out we either wake up or give up.

The dreams we once had shattered and crushed under the weight of reality, under the weight of a cruel world with people who can't wait to steal our dreams. Conformity wins. We see every mistake as a failure and our biggest fear is being vulnerable because we've associated that with being weak.

The things that happen to us thrive in shame. The shame we feel, because of the things we don't talk about or show, becomes the very chains that bind us.

I had promised myself a long time ago I would never be weak, I would never be hurt again. If I didn't let anyone close to me, it wouldn't hurt and I'd be a strong person that nothing could impact. I chose conformity on the outside but defiance on the inside.

And eventually I found myself in a story I didn't like and that I didn't intend to create. How did I get here? How did it all go so wrong? Like any great story it starts with a lost soul who must go on heroine's Journey.

It all came to boil the day I found myself sitting in a pool of protein shake on my kitchen floor, contemplating slicing my wrists to make the pain go away.

In this moment of darkness, the memories, decisions, choices, trauma all swirled around me. What others had done to me and what I had done to myself, blaming others for that too.

The pain was bubbling up inside of me and there was no escape. I had been through so much in my life. Why was this so different? Why couldn't I just shove it down anymore?

It was a battle of light and dark, of torment. Allowing myself to explore my darkness, my shame, and my resistance was the best gift I had given to myself. During my journey I heard an old Cherokee quote: *inside each of us is two wolves—a good and an evil and the one that wins, is the one we feed.* I stopped trying to make everything ok, I stopped pretending everything was ok. I let myself explore my dark side.

Instead of fearing it, I knew it would teach me. Exploring the darkness within me eventually drove the dark out. That dark wolf still lives inside of me, like it does inside you. We all have a shadow, a dark side. Trying to shut it out, trying to pretend it doesn't exist prevents us from learning from it. Allowing myself to go into those shadows allowed me to see what resentments and bitterness I was harboring.

Inside of that darkness was all of the things I had never dealt with. I no longer see it as the enemy. It's been my greatest teacher and continues to show me what needs to be looked at, what needs to be explored and what wounds need to be healed—where the light needs to get in.

The compartments in which I had been storing everything were blown open and I had to put it all back together. That's what this journey to the wild is about. From head to heart. From heart to soul.

NOTE TO READER

I didn't want to write this book. I didn't want to be the poster child for childhood sexual abuse. I didn't want that to be my story. I didn't want people to know.

I was scared of what it would mean for my life, my future, my family and what everyone would think. I wrestled hard between the wild that was coursing through my veins and my life, smashing everything inauthentic, every mask, wall, barrier that held me in some way, some version of protection that I was hanging onto and the need to keep those walls, that protection, that version of me that I had been for so long.

But then came that day in my kitchen, with an exploding protein shake and me on my knees. There was a fierceness that opened within me. I was climbing out of the most epic fall, a soul shattering, knees hitting the ground, broken open kind of fall. The kind where you have to go but you don't know if you'll ever be the same or ok again.

This was the first time I called myself a *wild soul woman*. I felt something inside of me awaken. There was a visceral, wildness, a sharpness of sight, hearing, and knowing, an awakening, a realness that I had never felt before.

I have never been the same.

When I was 9 or 10 years old, I don't know the exact age and I've never really asked about the dates, it was exposed that I had been sexually abused by an uncle for my whole life up to that point. I don't remember when it started, it was always just there. I don't remember when it stopped, but I will never forget the day it came out.

I pushed it down and decided then that I would never, ever talk about it again, impacting my life in ways I wouldn't understand for a long time, like struggling with an eating disorder for 20 years, among other things.

This book shares my story of coping (and not coping), healing (and re-healing) from childhood trauma. For me, my trauma stems from childhood sexual abuse, but this book isn't just about healing from sexual abuse. If you've experienced trauma of any kind, my hope is that you will find some hope in my story. Or maybe you know someone who has experienced trauma (you do, even if you don't know you do), and this book will help you understand their experience more and what they have to work through, overcome and how deeply they have to search for parts of themselves that were stolen and how deep they have to reach for their courage and faith.

We all have things happen. And we hide who we really are—we get lost. Unpacking it all is how we find our own inner wild woman. Change and healing is possible. I am living prove of that—of what's possible when we find redemption for ourselves, when we choose to become who we really are in spite of everything that's happened to us and to find our voice, our footing, our power in a world that wants to silence, cripple and destroy us.

In this book, my story will shift from past to present and not follow a particular timeline because the journey wasn't linear. What was happening today was interconnected to what happened in many areas of my life and many different ages. These journeys are like that…they don't care much about linear time.

As I unfolded the story, the mystery of me, and removed from the box the millions of pieces that I had never looked at, never processed, never felt, a bigger picture began to unfold and I could connect the dots of my life. Those dots and experiences didn't unfold in a linear story, which is why this book won't unfold in a linear fashion. I take you on the journey with me, from the cracks in the life I had been living to finding mindfulness and learning to process, to be in my life and finally, finding my voice that allowed me to really live my life instead of being a bystander, just merely existing.

As I share this extraordinary journey that took me from broken to brave, I want you to keep in mind your own stuff, your own bits, your own pain, your own trauma. The purpose of telling the story is to show what's possible when we choose to heal, no matter what your life or your story looks like, if I can find redemption, and choose to live fully, for myself then so can you. I just ask you to keep an open mind, allow yourself to play in possibility and be open to new concepts, new experiences.

What's mine is mine and if it fits for you, take it, use it, twist it, and own it. Embrace what speaks to your own wild soul and take your own journey.

This isn't an autobiography and its intention isn't to invoke pity or share a poor me story. The purpose of this book is to create a manual of sorts for others who are ready to reclaim their wild soul, who are ready to embark on their own journey and cut the cords that have bound them. Embarking on this journey can be scary and many people get stuck in various phases along the way. I hope this inspires you to see the phase you are in and continue on; because I promise you, the ending is worth the battle.

This is a story of unchaining myself from the story that there was something wrong with me and allowing myself to see myself for who I really am, not who I believed myself to be. What we hide hurts us. The things we bury come back to haunt us. We can't run forever.

The decision to write the book, to tell parts of my story didn't come easy. I know there will be judgement. I know there will be people who simply do not understand.

But I no longer care.

Because it's not about those people. The sharing of my story and my journey became something bigger than me, for people like me, people who have been through far too much to be contained in one book, people who became someone else, who hide themselves, dull themselves, live a life that causes us to die while we're still alive.

When I found the wild woman within, there was no going back.

PART 1

THE CRACKS
(Are How the Light Gets In)

There's only so much room under the rug before it can't take anymore. And if you allow yourself the privilege of "breaking down" you will breakthrough. Like a phoenix rising from the ashes, you will come back an even better stronger healthier version of you than you are now.
—Tonya Whittle

Chapter One

CRACK

What we hide hurts us.

In Japanese culture when something breaks they fill the cracks with gold. They don't deny the crack happened or wish to hide it. In fact, they make it pronounced, showing the beauty in the cracks by filling it with gold; the gold making it stronger than the original.

When a bone breaks, the place it healed is the strongest part of the bone.

Yet when it comes to broken hearts and broken lives we don't see these cracks as something beautiful or that which made us stronger. We see them as something to be ashamed of. Broken homes, broken lives, broken people; we don't want to look directly at it.

We stuff it down, we hide it away and we don't show our scars. Even though people us tell it's not our fault and to end stigma we need to talk about it, the truth is, most people are terribly uncomfortable with the truth. We'd rather a life of lies, we'd rather people pretend because then we can stay comfortable.

We fit the mold of what we're taught. We go along with what we're told, not what we feel. We don't fill our breaks with gold and say, "*look at this beautiful scar, something tried to kill me but I won*". Instead we wear them in silence and shame, hiding the things that made us who we are.

And we try to get as far away from the scars as possible and anything that will take us away from them we will do. We look to anything that can provide us with comfort because it's so much easier than sitting in the enormous pain.

We wear a mask and only show what we think we should, what we think will be liked, accepted and approved. We pretend we have it together and we show people what they want to see.

I didn't want to seem broken; I didn't want to be different. I didn't want to be pitied and I convinced myself that it didn't matter. It was fine; I was fine. I severed the connection to my wounds and didn't see that my behavior, who I had become, was connected to that at all.

I put things in a box, stuffed in the closet and left it there, where I felt it belonged, safe and not at risk of causing me embarrassment or shame. All I had to do was never ever let anyone close enough to find that box.

We like to look away from suffering because we have to remember our humanity when we're in close proximity to it. When we get up close to it it's hard to hate people when we see them, see their pain, see beyond what they show people and see who they really are.

We don't know what to do, what to say or what to make of it so we do nothing. Most of us are uncomfortable with the truth, with vulnerability. We live a closed life. We see what we want to see and we show people what we think is safe to show people.

We keep a safe distance and the very things we crave—Our basic human needs—certainty, variety, love/connection, significance, growth and contribution get met in unhealthy ways instead of the ways that will truly fill our soul.

I can get certainty from food or from knowing my purpose and believing that what I have experienced is for a reason.

I can get variety through drugs or alcohol or I can get it by deciding to change up my routine regularly, I can do different workouts or get involved with something I love to do—variety is about change.

Significance is the need to be important, to feel wanted and needed, to be unique. I can get significance from sleeping around; wanting to be wanted or I can get significance by knowing who I am and that my existence is important.

I can get deep passionate intimate love or I can settle for connection. Most people are too afraid of the big love, the deep love, the love that scares you, the love that opens you up to being hurt or even devastated should it end. Connection allows us to hide behind walls and settle for a lukewarm relationship—we get to be safe (certainty) and we get to feel protected and in control but we don't get to experience deep intimacy which is why we'll eventually experience suffering—because a need is not being met.

Growth is the need to grow, to learn and to move forward. It's one of the needs of the spirit and less of the human side and it's typically not a common need to be met until the other 4 are met. Contribution is the need to give beyond you. Another need of the spirit, contribution allows you to give to others with no expectation of anything in return.

Ultimately everything we do is for love but our needs structure is different from each other's and our life experiences and belief systems determine what things we'll use to meet these needs.

Someone who is driven to receive love but is too afraid to be vulnerable might choose to settle for connection or they may choose to get love by connecting with themselves when they eat.

Everything we do is to meet one of or more of these needs. I learned these through my studies and trainer to be a life coach, while also healing my own life. The higher the level of meeting these needs the bigger the addiction. If I'm using food to meet my needs for certainty and love and connection, it will meet the need but it will be an unhealthy way, which is why I'll feel temporary satisfaction but ultimately experience long-term pain from it. Because it will prevent me from having what I really crave—deep and unconditional love but my use of food will prevent me from going after what I really want.

When I smoked it met my needs for certainty, variety, connection all at the same time. In my early smoking days, it met my need for significance as well but as smoking became more shamed it wasn't meeting that need as I was hiding it and feeling shame for doing it.

Why? Because it met my needs in a way nothing else did. When I smoked I knew how I would feel—it would change my state, my moods in an instant. It would also provide variety by changing my mood as well as my location because I would have to go outside to do it. And it would provide connection—to myself for in those moments of smoking I was triggered to smoke by a bad mood and the cigarette was like a pacifier.

It allowed me to get away and escape from whatever was going on. With each inhale I would move further away from the issue and closer to the numb feeling I was craving so I could avoid the issue.

When we disconnect from our truth, from our stories, we disconnect from who we are. We wear masks to protect our stories, to appear whole but what we don't realize is that in denying our story we trade ourselves for "safer" versions.

Safer only in that they don't require us to be vulnerable, to be seen, to be naked in front of another; they do not require us to take a risk in being rejected or hurt or seen as less than, seen through the filter of our wounds.

Masking ourselves is not safer; it does not stop anything except the ability to live, to go after what we want. Masking doesn't serve us, doesn't serve the life we want to live, it just robs us of who we are—by hiding behind these stories, the omissions and the pretending that we do ultimately to hide the brokenness we feel.

It's sort of living, existing, as a shell of a person going through the motions and finding ways to cope that have nothing to do with what we're really craving—life. We can put all the pieces in place but it can't hide forever the façade that something isn't quite right—the right degrees, right house, right life when it's done to provide the image that you are whole when you have rejected yourself to create the image.

Those things are things outside of you and they will never fill the empty space you have inside that comes from denying your truth, rejecting who you are.

We become an observer to life, watching and measuring everything. We change who we are to fit, to blend in so our brokenness doesn't stand out, so we aren't pitied or rejected or looked at as though our broken pieces mean we are less than. If we amass enough of the right stuff that makes us successful then we can forget the blemishes.

But it will fill the hole for only a short time and you will feel the need for even more. It will not fill the emptiness you feel. The void that is inside of you will keep growing. It will only leave a voracious appetite for more so we can keep burying ourselves in stuff. Stuff cannot fix this void. Nor can keeping yourself "busy."

There is no space for your soul to speak to you, for that inner voice that tells you something is wrong, to wake up. I never had white space in my calendar. Even my drinking water was in there.

When I created my first vision board my coach asked me if I really wanted all of those things. I said no, but I had space so if it comes to me I'll be happy about it.

But in reality, I couldn't have space. I didn't want to hear the truth. I didn't like the voices that spoke to me, that told me something was off. I didn't know how to fix it, how to listen to it or what to do about it so it was better to just suffocate it so I couldn't hear it.

Being an adult was supposed to mean if I did all the right things then I'd be happy. I was able to make my own choices and didn't have to listen to anyone else. Where was my happily ever after? I was married and I felt like I had no idea who I was sleeping with. He sure didn't know me. I had a successful, sort of, business and was working for myself. I had the degrees, the house, the cars, and the pets.

I should have been happy. That's what the plan said. But underneath the amassing of the things, the letters, the papers, the numbers, was an undercurrent of proving myself that was driving me to do these things. I was living in avoidance, painting the picture of what I wanted to see and pretending that everything was great.

And then came the phone call.

The call came like I knew it would. You can't run from your past forever. Eventually it comes calling. I had pretended for so long, shoving it away into the recesses of my mind ignoring that this day would come. I wanted to hide it still. But I knew I couldn't. My new life was blissfully far away from my old life. And they were on a collision course.

My mother was on the other end of the line

"He's dying".

An uncomfortable silence followed, my mind catching up to what this meant for the life I had created that had nothing to do with *this*. How could I manage, mitigate, control this like I had been doing my entire life? Out of sight, out of mind and easy to hide.

I barely heard my mother as she said there will be a small funeral at the institution. I wasn't expected to go. They would spread his ashes "up home" (in reference to where they were originally from). I heard bits and pieces of things, feeling the floor spinning and a feeling of cotton balls engulfing me as I hung up the phone.

There was nowhere left to hide, but I looked for every possible out before I had to face it.

Chapter Two

EXPLOSION

I was consumed with the need to be successful that was driven by a fear of failing. And that was driven by my need to be significant, to be seen, to be important. I had never felt important or seen and this building and amassing degrees, business, clients, money, was all a way to prove to myself I was more than a statistic, that I was good enough.

At this stage of my life, I was involved in the fitness industry (owning my own studios). I was also burned out, exhausted, unable to say no, working 120-hour weeks to get it all done—anger and indignation were my fuel to get through my days. I never used excuses to not get things done, to not show up and not be 100% committed.

We all have an emotional home, a place we go, a place we spend a lot of time—it becomes our rocket fuel. I could get a lot of leverage and a lot of stuff done when I was angry. And I could find a lot of things to be angry about. I had become so triggered by things all I had to do was think about it and I was enraged.

The day of the exploding protein shake started in the typical manner. I was running late and feeling rushed. I yelled at my dogs to hurry up and walk, hurry up and eat. I raced to brush my teeth, wash my face and get my own breakfast at the same time, and suddenly I was covered in protein shake.

It was the final crack in a year of unbearable misery.

I had been through a lot of very messed up and painful things that year: the death of my abuser, feeling unsupported and disconnected in my marriage, feeling lost and alone all the time, business challenges and just a constant busyness and overwhelm that was bone aching and never ending. There were more things too, things I cannot talk about. Things that involve other people. Things that aren't only mine to share. But there were some deep things, big wounds busting open spilling out poison—while those should have broken me, they didn't.

But an exploding protein shake was the straw that broke the camel's back.

I forgot to put the lid on the blender and in that instant of explosion I felt something inside of me snap. Everything stopped and my grip on reality receded rapidly as I gripped the counter top white knuckled. I couldn't take anymore. I could feel the rage bubbling inside of me. I couldn't contain it.

Why I screamed. *Why did everything have to go wrong? Why can't anything go right* I yelled into the air? The dogs were frightened. This wasn't their first witnessing of a breakdown, but it was the worst one. I could feel the simmering rage and I didn't want to contain it.

The hot tears sprung to my eyes, I was barely holding on. I fought them back. I could feel everything spinning as my rage and anger grew and all I could think about was how completely messed up my life had gotten and I couldn't see an end. I wanted it to end.

I knew in that moment that I needed an out. I couldn't go on like this. I began to have images of taking my own life, putting my car off the road, a knife to my skin, anything to make the pain go away—it could be over so quickly, as my hand came to rest on the handle of a knife sitting on the counter.

My thoughts were interrupted when Tetley, my chocolate Labrador retriever, barked violently. We locked eyes, and I knew she understood where my mind was wandering. I slid down the counter too angry, too frustrated and too exhausted to cry. She buried her head in my neck and I held onto her lion's mane of fur. There we were, locked in the only embrace I could receive, in front of the only ones I could show this breakdown. I wouldn't dare let anyone else see me that way.

My other chocolate lab, Lexie Lou, who was rescued from an abusive home, was my softness dog, she was the one who forced me to slow down, she had just come into my life and was a challenge in ways that showed the stark contrast between my life and her needs. She was traumatized. She was slow. She was soft. She was healing just in her presence. She was all the things I wasn't and everything I needed. That day she lay her head in my lap, pushing her weight into me.

As I lay there, the decisions I had made in my life, who I had become and what was happening in my life washed over me. I couldn't move. My mind was racing, heart palpitating, everything both sharp and dull at the same time. I was in a vortex, my life a mess that I had never been able to see.

Who am I? Why is my life like this? How did it all get so effed up? It wasn't supposed to be like this. I wanted something different. I dreamed of something different. But here I am, making decisions I know I'll regret, choosing things I don't want over things I do want, too scared to say no, too scared to yes. Too scared to speak up and ask for what I want. Too scared and jaded to admit what I really wanted. I don't even know what I was doing or how I was living, I was just doing all the time, without thought or reflection.

How had things gone so wrong? This wasn't what I wanted to create. I had just wanted to help people. I wanted to be healthy and help others live a healthy life and here I was living a life of exhaustion and rage—frustrated with everyone and everything around me, my own life was a mess. I wanted to run but I didn't know where to go. I wanted to escape, to leave it all behind.

God, there had to be a way out, right? Why I was talking to God all of a sudden. Did he exist? Was there even a God? If there was, why was everything so screwed up?

Are we just meant to suffer and die? Is there a bigger purpose to all of this? Here I was trying to make something of myself, taking chances, trying to help people and I felt worse off for trying. Could I give up? I owed too much money to quit now. I'm not sure what I was even striving for? If I got all the things, the checklist I had in my mind, that would mean I was successful and mean I wasn't what I feared I was—broken and damaged.

Proving myself had gotten worse since I had met my husband. I seemed to so easily listen to him, let him lead all the time, let him tell me what to do and how to be, what was important and what wasn't, I was constantly trying to please him in a way that cost me myself.

In the early days of our relationship I changed into what he wanted me to be. He liked "sporty" girls, so I wore more fitness wear. He didn't like my bang, so I changed it. At the time they seemed so innocent, not big things at all, but looking back over the landscape it's easy to see where it started—liking him and wanting him to like me to. But he didn't like *me*. He didn't know me. I became what he wanted, what he liked, what he approved of instead of being myself. Or at least, what I thought he wanted me to be. I never bothered to say "too bad". Or "this is me". Instead I just changed for what I thought he wanted.

Anytime something happened that upset me or I didn't feel good about, I stuffed it down and went along, ignoring alarm bells, warning signs, comments and so much more.

I waited for his permission and approval for everything. I shrunk inside of myself more and more and stopped asking for anything, stopped showing up in our relationship really. I was there, but I wasn't really there. I think I was waiting for him to show up. I was waiting for something. I don't even know what it was.

I wanted to be there and when he wasn't, I didn't ask, didn't push, didn't want to be "that girl". I always felt like I wasn't enough or couldn't measure up somehow. Because of my ability to just turn off, I don't know what I was thinking or feeling most of the time.

I just shut down. I hit the off button, escaping from having to do or say anything.

And here I was, sitting on the floor, arms around my dog with another on my lap, exhausted, overwhelmed, unhappy, frustrated and just back against the wall feeling. The pain of who I had become, the things I let happen to me, the ways I behaved myself, how I showed up, the failures, the judgements, all of it bubbled up, and I realized I couldn't do this anymore.

Lying on the kitchen floor came on the heels of a horrible year. Everything that could go wrong went wrong. I didn't know it then, but there was a lot worse to come. I would be propelled into a journey that I couldn't have stopped if I wanted to and wouldn't have done if I had been given an itinerary.

Car doors signaled my clients' arrival for their group training sessions in my private studio in my house. I owned 2 fitness studios at that time and was working both locations. I wasn't a business owner; I was a business operator. And I wasn't doing a good job of it, spread too thin over too many tasks, this was the result.

I cleaned up as best I could and for the first time decided to just be honest with my clients as I told them, making it funny, about my protein shake experience. We all laughed but only I knew how close to not getting off the floor I was.

Chapter Three

SPACE

Something shifted inside of me that day. I had been questioning a lot of things for some time but I wouldn't let myself look too closely at anything. I didn't know what to do with it, how to face it so I kept pushing it away.

I was questioning my marriage. I was angry. We had been through a lot—I felt he didn't choose me, often choosing his own interests over me, leaving me behind and even speaking to me without respect in his voice. We had unresolved issues and I felt this enormous space between us and no room to speak up or talk about it. I traded my voice for peace, for choosing the easy way, to not stir the pot, I shoved it all down.

I felt like everything was my fault. I was on eggshells all the time.

My business had become something other than I had wanted it to be and I wasn't sure what was the truth with my marriage anymore, I was frustrated, overwhelmed and wondering what are we *doing*? I wondered if we were on the same path anymore.

But then we didn't really know each other anymore. All I did was work. We didn't see each other, eat together, connect because work had taken over my life.

Things had gotten all tangled up and I didn't know what to do. I didn't know how I had gotten into the mess I was in but I felt trapped. All the things I had always pushed under the rug didn't seem to fit like they used to anymore. I was aware I wasn't dealing with it. Long gone were the blissfully days of living in denial.

During class that day I remarked that perhaps it was time to look at how busy my life was because I was always so rushed I couldn't function, everything was half done and I was overwhelmed with it all.

And divine intervention, I suppose, happened.

A client of mine taught mindset training. I said I didn't have time to sing along to kumbaya and hug each other. She told me that it was simply a way of seeing things differently that could help me not be so reactive in life. So, I decided I would go to this event and see if it could provide something to help with how I was feeling. I was a yes person and since I had just said I needed something, I didn't want to say no.

And my life was forever changed for it.

Not because of that one course, none of us are "fixable" in one thing. The work we have to do for our internal wellness takes practice and time. But the concepts introduced were life altering to me in that moment, understanding our thoughts was the biggest concept, as I had never heard anything like it and it set me on a journey that led me down many paths and roads that ultimately helped me get where I am today. It was the start of something.

The cracks are how the light gets in, our moments of weakness, vulnerability, uncertainty and allowing ourselves to be honest and show how we are really feeling that leads us to deeper and more profound connections to others and ourselves. Pretending we have it all together is the thing that prevents us from finding ways to get it together, to learn and grow.

We are so afraid to let people see we might have made a mistake or gotten in over our heads or that we don't know something because we're afraid of what it will mean about us. The reality is that our inability to admit we need help, that we're not ok is the very thing that will help us get the tools we need. But perfection holds us hostage. Fear of rejection; of our scars being exposed holds us prisoner to these masks, never about to stand up and say "*look, this is me. This is my life. This is my experience and I'm hurting.*" We become prisoners, trapped in a world of our own creation.

This workshop gave me a new way of looking at things and gave me peace, even bliss for a time, to see things so differently, to realize that I really was in control and that I could change how I viewed things. And it was only possible because I had decided to tell the truth. The truth was that I wasn't happy doing what I had been doing. I was running a business that no longer gave me joy but was adding immense stress in my life. My work was all consuming and I wanted more. I was not home with my husband, ever. And the fulfillment I wanted in my life was lost because of how addicted to work I had become.

When I arrived at the event I was stressed and nervous, I hadn't taken more than a day off in years. I had to reschedule 2 complete days to be here and I wasn't sure what to expect. I didn't have a lot of information on what this would be about, except to come with an open mind. All of the conferences I had attended were for a specific purpose—upgrading, learning, cec's, new certifications—not personal development.

While this course helped me get started and I left feeling blown open and amazing, a new outlook and fresh start on life, I eventually moved away from a lot of its concepts and worked more deeply on emotions, health and how trauma is stored in the body, deep soul work and shamanic healing became a bigger focus, as I believe mindset alone can keep us trapped in unhealthy cycles.

For me, I had been pushing everything down, painting it with a different brush, justifying, cleaning up other people's side of the road, and mindset work alone helped me continue that behavior. Moving deeper into emotions and soul work helped me overcome it and reclaim the power that I had been giving away my entire life.

But at the time of this event, I held no joy in my life. I was always rushing from one thing to the next. I was angry, frustrated, annoyed and overwhelmed every single day. I felt like a failure in every area of my life—as a wife, as a dog mom, as a daughter, an aunt, a friend, as a coach, a business owner.

The happy life image was starting to crumble as I looked closer at what I had built. Thus far I had been able to pretend, I was able to explain it all away, put it in nice box and label it and tell myself whatever made me feel better.

Being busy allowed me to not deal with anything I didn't like. I could pretend I didn't see it.

But it was there, creating cracks all over the place, a spider web of cracks had started from that phone call and I didn't see it until it shattered into a pool of protein shake. I didn't see the full connection of that phone call for years.

The light had gotten in and I couldn't help but see things differently.

But I kept putting my head down, trying to hold the flood at bay by fixing all the surface problems. If I could fix my business I'd have more time with my husband and that would help. If I could make more money, I could take more time off and everything would be ok.

I was always trying to prove to him that I was enough and I blamed myself for not being there as much. I blamed myself for creating the stress of starting a business.

No matter what happened, I took responsibility for it all. I blamed my business and myself. If I could just fix that, things would be fine.

I did that in all areas of my life. Blamed myself. I always found a way to come back to it being my fault.

I was building a business at a cost of my life. I lived to work. There was no me outside of work. During that first mindset course I realized I had just become an extension of the business. I no longer knew how to have fun or communicate with people if it wasn't in relation to my work.

Who was I without this label, this identity of a trainer, a coach, a nutritionist who helped people get results lived a perfectionist life— afraid to not be perfect because then I wouldn't be "good enough". So, I lived a life of no mistakes, no fun—I had a professional image to uphold. I lived it as though my life depended on. I didn't exist outside of the business.

While I never blamed him for anything in our marriage, I went from wearing rose colored glasses to wearing glasses that blocked all the good. I just saw problems everywhere. With us, my business, my life, everyone and everything.

Back then, I never looked at what it must have been like, to live with someone who isn't there, who isn't available. I don't know if either of us was actually emotionally available. Maybe that's why this had been working in some twisted way for so long. Instead of looking at myself I was looking at him. Isn't that what we're so good at?

As I began to relax, unwind after that seminar I was in love with the idea of mindset and I realized just how much mindset had played a role for me without me knowing it back when I changed my life nearly 10 years before and what had led me into the fitness industry.

I realized this was the missing piece of what I had been looking for. I wanted to teach how I had changed my mindset and changed my life with eating disorders and how I went to from full of excuses to full of commitment but I hadn't known how to get others to change too.

My shift had come literally as though someone planted thoughts in my head that I had no idea where they came from. I weighed myself every day. I didn't want to go to work most days because I felt fat.

One particular morning when I was 24 years old, 10 years earlier, I was standing on the scale I felt the familiar shame of having regained weight. I had been super skinny from not eating for a time and now I had gained it all back, again. I was infuriated. I felt the sting of shame and the overwhelming feelings that always followed the weight gain after a vicious cycle of starvation. As I sat on my bed feeling sorry for myself, wanting to call in sick to work but not allowing myself to, I had a thought that I had to change my life.

I knew profoundly that this was no way to live life—everything shadowed by my weight. What if I was never skinny? What if I never experienced happiness? What if I let this be my life forever? How long could I reasonably live like this before either dying from the illness or dying from the mental anguish from it.

I knew I had to change my thoughts—which I had to become healthy and focus on positive change. I knew that I had to change my language. I didn't know where these thoughts had come from but I knew they were true. I followed them and it changed my life. Despite helping people in fitness for more than 6 years I was realizing understanding how to explain how to change to people was what I was actually trying to do all along. I wanted people to have control over their lives like I had gotten from changing my mindset, changing how I viewed things. I actually had sources, resources and ways to learn even more.

I had gotten side tracked from that purpose and I had become what the fitness industry taught me to be. See the pattern? I became what I thought others wanted. Not even necessarily what they told me to be, but what I assumed they wanted.

I had gotten obsessed with getting people physical results and I had lost my own mindset about health to the industry that is about looks and not health.

This new conversation showed me how I had strayed from my own beliefs. I violated my values to meet my need for significance—being important to people, having my photos posted and finally becoming the "hot girl" I always wanted to be. I got off my path so I could revel in that.

I traded my passion for short-lived fame.

I began to see how my mindset was impacting my business and I began to shift and change things. I was sure I could turn it around.

It was also easier to focus on the business, fixing the business than too look closely at my personal life. It was too raw, too uncomfortable, too much that I didn't know what to do with. I again looked away and convinced myself that my business was the most important thing I had to fix.

I now know I wasn't meant to turn it around. The cracks had spread too far. The damage was done—I couldn't keep operating at the hours I was pulling in order to fix the mess it had become.

I also didn't want to. I was done. That was the real truth. I had set it up in a way that was fueling and feeding burn out. I didn't know who I was. I had no idea what I stood for. Fear ruled my decisions and I was focused on what wasn't working, meltdowns and anger became my best friends.

While I finally had amazing staff after years of struggling to find people who had the same work ethic, values and beliefs that I held, I had nothing left to give to the business. I was done. I was finished, exhausted. I didn't have it in me to continue. I had been working 2 and 3 jobs since college. I believed if I pushed hard enough it would work. I believed if I did enough, if I worked enough hours, if elbow grease could fix it, then I could do it.

But I couldn't. I had depleted myself. I was emotionally, mentally, physically exhausted. I had developed eating disorders, again. I had been well for years, sure that I would never go back there again, but being in the fitness industry and living a life where your looks are judged daily, competing in fitness competitions, believing that my worth was equal to my body fat percentage, I developed food neurosis, body dysmorphia, over training and self-hate.

And I had no life. I wanted to live! I wanted to spend time with family, friends and reconnect with my husband. We had something special, I knew that in my soul, but life and trauma and drama was in between us.

Now that I had taken the rose-colored glasses off I knew I had to let go. I wasn't in the place to fix this, to continue to teach this. My next steps meant I had to let go and let myself heal, let myself rest and let myself learn why I had gotten here, again. How had this happened?

I knew that answering that question would ultimately help me help many people. It was not the time to build the business in the way I had been trying to. It was time to let go and find a new way.

More importantly, it was time to find me.

The cracks could not be ignored any longer. There were too many things not working in my life and I had found tools and skills to help me face it all and turn things around.

So, I let the biggest crack come. I closed my studio that I just opened. I was going to lose a lot of money but I knew if I didn't change it now while I still had a choice, I would be forced to change it. I couldn't handle the stress and I needed to get out and heal my own life.

I allowed myself to be honest again. I did what was best for me, for the business as a whole. It was the first time I had decided on my own. I hadn't told my husband. I did talk to coaches about it but ultimately, I sat with the decision and it was the first time I had listened to my soul. Hand on heart.

And the answer was to get out. To let go.

I didn't have anything to give anyone. I needed to be filled up. So, I told the staff, the clients, and I found a buyer. Giving up wasn't easy but I knew holding on was going to be harder. I was no longer willing to give up my life for this. This studio had been a band aid to a bigger problem.

The day the sale became final I reflected on so many things. I knew something dramatic had happened. I felt immediate relief. I knew in my soul I had made the right decision.

Without the worry of the business and the overwhelm of staff, it was just me and an open road. I was ready for this new phase, this new task—armed with nearly a year of personal development, a new business coach and a willingness to move forward, I was ready to tackle the world and get back to creating the business I had always wanted to create while healing myself and reclaiming my life.

I started with the question of my eating disorder, how had I gotten here again? I felt raw as I looked at my eating disorders with the enormous tasks of understanding them. I had "fixed them" but I had never really understood why I had them. And I knew I had to go there— to understand what caused them and my obsession with my body.

With less stress my eating became more structured, healthier on its own. Reinforcing the belief that stress is a leading cause of food problems. I was using food to cope—or in my case—restriction, lack of food, controlling food. The pain I got in my stomach felt like control.

I liked that feeling. It was certainty. But it was not good control. It was an old behavior from childhood. I had become obsessed with my weight at 8. I started my first diet when my mom bought diet books through my schoolbook order. Can we all take a moment to appreciate growing up in a world where diet books are sold in children's schoolbook program?

A moment of silence for all the girls who learned as a child their looks, their bodies, their weight was all they were worth.

I read them on the bus on the way home. I started measuring my collarbone structure. I was obsessed with counting my ribs. By the age of 16 I had a full-blown eating disorder—starvation with binge and purge bouts.

I was addicted to laxatives and was in enormous pain when I didn't take them.

Sitting in a doctor's office waiting for an eye specialist appointment—I had cut my eye in a freak accident in school—I was experiencing immense pain in my stomach. I asked my mother for laxatives and she asked why I needed them. I told her I was constipated and she made a reference of me throwing up and was I using them for that? I said no.

She knew.

I suppose they had no idea what to do about it. I was a master liar at this age. Having learned to just lie straight faced about anything that might be shameful or that would get me in trouble. I was a good-hearted person but if it meant being "found out" I was going to lie until I went to my grave.

Food had been a way to focus on something else, focus on my body, on perfecting myself, on controlling things when things were out of control. And it always seemed like things were out of control.

I never tried to control anyone else…just myself. I liked how this felt. In an out of control world, this was the one thing I could control. My need for certainty trumped all else and instead of meeting that need in a healthy way I did it in an unhealthy way.

Realizing this, I was able to release some of that pressure. No wonder I felt the need to restrict food with the business being unstable, dealing with staff, and all the things that come with running a business when you have no idea what you're doing or when you realize you've bitten off more than you can chew and feeling like it was all I had.

With less stress I automatically felt better and things fell into a sort of natural rhythm. I didn't think too much about food. I was eating well but I wasn't happy with my body. I was still striving for more and better in that area.

Signing up for fitness competitions triggered my eating disorders again, and since I stopped competing, I couldn't seem to maintain a healthy weight and I was fluctuating greatly.

I couldn't get that stoic resolve I'd always been able to find. I had always been able to double down, just lock it into place, but that was gone now.

I wanted to feel healthy, happy, vibrant, and strong in my body again. But I did not. I knew things would get better with my body and since so many other things were looking up, I let it slide. I put it to the side and focused on other more important matters.

Letting go of part of my business gave me space, breathing room, space where I didn't have to work nonstop or be on all the time. I didn't care that I was going to lose my investment. In hindsight, I know I made rash decisions. I didn't always plan properly. Looking back, I realize how often I just acted without thinking, moving, running, all the time.

But this move, was the right one. I knew it was time to let go.

I wanted to spend time with my husband, get to know him again, to spend time with friends and mostly focus on my own wellbeing. I knew I wasn't in a position to keep pushing forward. I had some big questions to answer. I wanted to know why my eating disorders came back. I wanted to know how I had gotten "here". I wanted to know more and I wanted to know myself.

I couldn't do that without space, time, and energy. I left it behind and spent the next year working on my mindset, uncovering the root cause of my eating disorders, repatterning my behavior, spending time on me again, in my life not outside of my life. I was falling in love with life again and life was falling in love with me.

With my business coach, I was learning the psychology of business, the mindset it took to be in business and I was learning a lot about who

I was as a business owner and creating a business that I really wanted. I was laying the groundwork for the business I wanted to create.

I had never done these things before. A whole new world was opening to me and I was excited about where I was going. Some down time, new lessons, exciting plans for the future.

Life was about to be awesome!

I could see a new path forward and I was confident I could find a way to create it all. I had created space in my life and it felt good. For the first time in a long time I was excited for the future. I had a life and a successful business and a plan.

Creating space not only created room for life, it created room for memories, for hopes and dreams. So much had shifted for me I didn't realize how little shifted in my outside world.

I felt like a new person on the path to where I was heading— revamping my business with the confidence and the knowledge to step into my destiny.

It never occurred to me that I hadn't even yet begun my journey, that I was merely preparing for my journey. I used to joke that I didn't have time for the breakdown I needed to have. But as it turns out, I had just created about 60 hours a week in my schedule.

Some of that white space I hated.

Chapter Four

BREAKDOWN

thought it had all been so hard up to now. The healing hadn't even begun and I was racing to the finish line of where I was going to end up, again. I began to form a new vision of where I would go now that I had found my missing puzzle piece.

I worked diligently all that year to clean up the mess. I felt as if my eating disorder, my mindset, my outlook was significantly improving. I was happier and felt less stressed, even if I didn't have all the things or the pieces.

Nine months into this new journey I took my first solo trip. At this point in my life, things had been going well, my husband and I were getting to know each other again, spending more time together. I was home working all the time with no places to rush off and he had lost his job as the company he worked for went bankrupt.

That might seem like a lot of things going horribly wrong but in reality it was the biggest gift we had been given. It gave us time to come together, spend time together, to get to know each other again.

So, when I jumped on a plane and headed for Las Vegas for a business conference, I did so excited to take things to the next level. I knew if I could figure out the business piece then I'd be able to really relax and enjoy life even more.

During this business conference I soon discovered that I was the problem. I really never pictured myself as a victim but I now realized I was playing the full-blown victim in my business.

I didn't realize that who I was showing up as was creating the problems I had in my business. I always thought it was external problems I had to fix, and I would fixate on the problem. What someone else wasn't doing or not doing. I told the story of no one caring over and over again.

My world was shaken. *I* was the problem. The decisions *I* made. *My* reactions. *My* behaviors. Everything that had gone wrong in the business was a sum total of who I was and what I believed in. What I believed in was how I showed up and what I expected. And I expected to be let down. I expected people to not show up. I expected things to go wrong. I expected to not be supported.

I was excited and yet thrown for a loop. I had no idea what to do with this information. *I was responsible.* The business was what it had become as a result of who I was.

So, who was I?

A team member from the conference and I had impactful conversation on my last night there about life, business, and how it all blended and what it was all for. He left me with these parting words: "I hope the man in your life knows how amazing you are and how incredibly lucky he is to have you."

Suddenly my world spun from underneath me. I heard his words but even louder was a thrumming in my head. Deep in my soul I thought,

I'm the one who needs to see how amazing I am. Not him. This isn't about him or anyone else. This is about me. Why couldn't I see my worth or how amazing I am?

Why did I look in people's eyes and see the worst of my reflecting back? Why did I think it was all my fault? Why did I always think I was broken, messed up, not good enough?

Why would I discredit a stranger' words? Someone I had been in conference with and met briefly who could see into me but yet those I spend the most time with could not?

The air left my body as I realized I didn't let people I knew see me. I was still being some version of me that I thought was safe, closed off, didn't care and wasn't available.

Why was I so closed at home and so open with people I didn't know—because they didn't know me. I didn't have a reputation, an agenda, an image to protect. I could be me. I could be open. I could let myself out, let down walls down, and just be myself. I wasn't worried about being hurt.

My business was not the thing that needed to be fixed, my life was. I had to face all the things that were going on in my personal life. I wondered now, had I been keeping myself busy in business to avoid my personal life and pretending I didn't want the things I did want? Was I staying busy so no one could get close to me? Was I holding everyone at bay?

Why could I not see what others saw? Why could I not believe I was incredible, or awesome or any of those things? I felt so uncomfortable with someone saying I was worth more.

My life was flashing before my eyes and I was struggling to keep myself together. I felt a thousand cuts from everything I had been through, everything I experienced that I never really let myself experience or feel because I always found a way to blame myself for it and then swallow it down, shove it into a box and close it off where it was more comfortable.

Was this what it was like to die? Cause it sure felt like it.

All the things I refused to look at, the things I said were ok, the things I pushed away and continued on my path were surfacing *now.*

I felt sick so I bid my goodbyes to my team, went to my room to collect my luggage. I had one hour left in Vegas and I spent it sobbing in my room.

It was the first time I cried in so long I couldn't remember. Tears were not something I did. I bottled everything up and held onto it. Now it was pouring out of me.

I had come here excited for moving my business forward but in the snap of a finger I had no idea what was happening anymore. I was armed with the knowledge of how to run a business but I had a gaping hole in my life.

I felt as if someone set off dynamite inside me. Something short circuited and everything I had put in the closet had exploded out on the floor. I stared at it all, moment after moment washing over me, engulfing me in pain.

I felt fractured.

As I headed home I picked up a pack of cigarettes. I had no idea what to do with this so I did what I always did—I stopped eating and started smoking. It was the coping tool I had so I didn't completely lose my mind...but here I was, again, now seeing myself make these decisions, knowing I was coping but seemingly unable to stop it.

Chapter Five

OFF

I returned home from the conference a different person. I had left so excited but I returned angry, feeling different toward my husband and family. I felt raw and everything that brushed up against me felt like it was pulling a million strings attached to a million knives.

I had accepted so little in my life and I was pushing through life, trying to fix everything on the outside to make it all better, to make it all right, but I couldn't fix the outside stuff until I fixed the inside stuff.

I was about to go ahead and create the exact same thing in business that I had already created and left behind. This new information forced me to come back and deal with the things I needed to deal with before moving on and creating something else that I wasn't meant for.

I didn't want to go there. I wanted it to be about my business. I wanted to have that to fix. I didn't want it to be about me. It was clear how much I had spent working on work and not on my life and I didn't want to see all the problems in my life. I didn't know how to fix those.

When we look at where we spend our time we can see what we're making a priority. I used to say I was working to create a better life for my husband and I. But if my husband was so important to me why wasn't I spending time with him?

I too busy trying to prove myself worthy to get his love, always looking for validation and approval.

But why did I need him to give me that? Why did I go, like a child with a new drawing, waving it for approval? Look what I did. And it was never fulfilling. Because when we seek approval and enoughness in someone or something else it will always feel like it's not enough. I would sink it down into the box with the other things, not realizing that until I saw myself as enough, that I could never get that void filled from another.

More More More. When would it ever be enough? What did I want? Why did I need his approval, his permission? And permission of everyone outside of me? It wasn't just him. It was my parents, family, friends and clients.

Who am I? What have I created? Am I crazy? The conversations spun over and over in my head. Flipping every minute from justification to denial.

I had this convenient off switch. This off button that let me ignore feelings, signs, and warnings that something was wrong. I could look directly at things and not see them, convince myself of something else and go completely somewhere else—most often work or a new project, something to distract me, the shiny object syndrome. Escaping was my super power.

I'm not sure I knew I was doing it at the time. I had this identity of me, of who I was, and saying anything, being needy, weak, vulnerable was not included in that identity. I was the don't give a f*** girl.

I reminded and reinforced my identity of not needing anyone, and it not mattering. I never asked for more. I never stood up for myself. I just went along with it. I shoved it down and painted the picture the way I wanted it to be in my mind, devoid and avoiding reality.

I can't say I was ever really upset by things. I don't know how I was back then, completely unconscious to the decisions I made, the things I believed and how I lived my life. Reflecting back, it's hard to remember just how toxic, angry, complaining, frustrated I was. I remember it but it's like it was all happening to someone else.

And really, it was. I can hardly remember what it felt like because back then I didn't feel anything. I was a shell.

I never stopped to assess anything. If I didn't like it got chucked in the box in the closet and I closed the door on it and went onto something else. There was no conscious thought to anything.

Now I was feeling everything at once. I kept convincing myself it didn't matter, that it was all in the past and there wasn't nothing that could be done to change any of it, so why bring this stuff up now?

I kept pushing it away but it kept coming up. I was annoyed and frustrated all the time. I was trying to think positive, fake it till I made it, looking for the gratitude. I had always been able to turn off but it seemed impossible now. I was sinking in misery and the more I pretended the worse I felt.

PART 2

MINDFULNESS

What defines us is how well we rise after we fall.

Chapter Six

VISION

One of my favorite activities is running because I could just turn myself off. Block out thoughts and just focus on the run. One foot in front of the other. Embrace the calm that overtakes me where no thoughts exist.

While out on a run one day, about a month after I'd returned home from Vegas, something frightening happened; I had a vision.

I was projected into the future where I was speaking at an event about being a sexual abuse survivor. As quickly as it had happened, it was over, I stopped so suddenly that I left drag marks in the dirt. I felt like a wild animal being hunted.

My senses were on fire, I felt it was the truth and I was at the same time trying to back away from it but unable to escape. Why would I think that? What just happened? That didn't feel like thinking, it felt like

I was somewhere else, in another time and another place. It felt real, and I was terrified. An avid and lifelong over thinker, this experience was not merely thinking. It was as though I just simply wasn't there.

I wanted to scream and laugh and cry at the same time. *NEVER, ever would I speak publicly about that.* I was fine. It was a long time ago. He was dead. Bad things happen and we all have to decide if we're going to let it impact us or not.

A long time ago I had decided I would never let it be my story. It would not be relevant to my life and I would not let it impact me. I put it in the box, stuck in the closet, denied it happened and moved on.

Where was this coming from? Why was this coming up?

My grasp on reality was loosening and I could feel a descent into madness that wouldn't begin to lift for more than a year. I was pulled into a vortex where everything I had ever experienced was swirling.

Spiraling was a nice word for where I was. Opening the box on that memory, that feeling, that thing that happened that I didn't intend to ever go into, was crushing me.

I was struggling with basic tasks. And I was so angry. Angry at everyone, angry at the world. My mouth was no longer zipped. I couldn't contain my rage, my frustration, my irritation. Everything bothered me and I couldn't swallow it anymore.

My edges and angles became sharp. I felt like I was drowning in one sense and getting up, showering, buttering my toast, driving to appointments, talking to clients, eating dinner, folding laundry.

It was as though there was suddenly two of me. The me that was kicking and clawing her way out and the me that was shoving her back down screaming at her to not to be so stupid and to not ruin everything.

I was going through the motions on the outside but fighting demons on the inside. I didn't know what to do. I was struggling. This time I couldn't find the walls to get behind or the box to shove it in. In fact, when I went looking, the box was wide open and its bits spilled all over the floor.

I was looking at things differently. How much I didn't stand up for myself, ask for what I wanted, speak the truth. I noticed how uncomfortable I was all the time. I became aware of my own duality. And even more so I became aware of a painful reality that I was living but had painted all the colors of the rainbow.

I knew it was there. I had felt that truth over the last few years but this was an ultimate shattering, knees on the ground, hands down, back arched, painful sobs bursting from my tired soul, kind of down.

I didn't know how to get up from this.

Chapter Seven

MEDIATE

Wanting to help me relax and maybe gain some tools to help with my frequent meltdowns, my business coach invited me to a meditation circle.

I was scared. Looking back now it was so strange to be so terrified to go a meditation class. That will tell you just how closed I was. They invited me to bring something to place on the alter and I was literally freaking out. Is this a cult? A church? What have I gotten myself into? I had already done some wild stuff over the past 2 years but this was getting really wacky.

I had committed and didn't want to cancel so off I went, empty handed as I had no intentions of putting anything on any alter, fully armed with my trusty ability to not be there while being there. It was a small group in someone's living room. The alter turned out to be a cloth where candles were lit and you could place something special to infuse with good energy.

I had overreacted slightly.

But I still wondered what my husband, my parents, my family would think if I they saw me there. Did I really need this? Or did I just need to brush it all off and get back to my life? This was all a big distraction from doing what I needed to do.

We meditated and shared. And repeated that process several times. I didn't experience much. I couldn't relax well. I didn't like "letting go" in groups of people. I found it difficult to relax, even sleep, when I was around unfamiliar people, even people I knew. It was a constant struggle to turn off my fear, the always on guard part of me.

I focused on breathing and suddenly I was somewhere else, again. I felt myself slipping away; I was in a pit of darkness, floating. I was trapped, clawing to get free, I couldn't breathe, scrambling.

I began to float above it, staring at this giant pool of darkness, a black cloud and I knew instantly that everything I had ever experienced that I had not dealt with was in there. These questions I had been asking lately, who am I? Why am I like this? What do I want? Why do I do what I do?

The answers to everything I wanted to know, even the eating disorder, the smoking, the off button; it was all in there.

It was enormous. I felt the weight of it on my body, my shoulders, my soul. I was overwhelmed and exhausted just seeing it. I also knew I had to go into it. And I was terrified of what was in there.

So much had happened. I had turned off so long ago that I didn't remember most of it, but it was there. I had no idea where to find the on button but I had a sneaking suspicion it was in that black hole.

I wasn't sure I was strong enough to go through that heaping pile of garbage. Could I face it? What would I find, what if I couldn't handle it and it broke me?

I had withdrawn so far inside of myself I didn't know who I was or why I was doing what I was doing. I was just trying to get through each day, hoping it would all come together at some point. I was going through the motions of living. In fact, I wasn't really living at all.

And now, it seemed more problems, more questions, more stuff, more heaviness, more emotions. I was frustrated that this journey was taking so long and as soon as I had a path to focus on moving toward, the rug was pulled out, again.

As I lay on the floor that day, next to the "alter" in the small living room with a group of women, I felt both heavy and light. I knew that so much of my pain, feeling trapped and stuck, unable to move forward, were in that black hole. It was a relief to know where it was—all the memories I couldn't locate, all of the gaps in my life, all of the emotions I never felt, all of the experiences I struggled with. But it was also heavy, knowing that I had to face it, that I had to go into it, that I would have to explore that giant darkness.

But, I just wanted to move forward with my plans but I could barely get up in the mornings. I started hitting snooze, was spending the day in my pj's and chain smoking. This was a vicious cycle but at least before I was showing up in the life, now I wasn't showing up, I was hiding.

I didn't know where to go from here. What was I supposed to do with all of this? While the meditation group opened up another world to me, I had no idea where to start with this. I was working with a business coach at the time and while she wasn't an expert in this field, she knew a lot about this world that I had not yet navigated. My coach, Jennifer Trask, was the one person who was had a front row seat into what was unfolding in my life.

On the outside, I was mum about what I was experiencing and going through, not even sharing with my husband the things I was struggling with, worried about making everyone else comfortable and keeping up appearances at all costs, Jennifer the one person I wasn't hiding from.

She had front row tickets to the epic fall that was happening as I was untangling who I had become and finding who I was. She is, still to this day, perhaps the only person who could really appreciate the change from where I was to where I am. She is the only person who bore witness to the entire journey.

She recommended I get a session with a local healer. I didn't know going there that she would be "reading me"—reading my energy, reading my life basically, like a psychic but not like a psychic. A channeler, a reader, a healer, a sage. I didn't know what to expect.

I had gone to a card reader for fun some years before and he was scarily accurate so I never thought about it again, as one would who was living a closed off life of denial.

I could write a book on her reading alone. I was skeptical. I wanted it to be over before it was even started and I again found myself wondering if I was just losing my mind. Having a family history of mental illness, I was beginning to wonder if I had drawn the short straw. I was terrified that I was insane and that my life was heading down a path of inability to cope or function in the real world.

When she landed on my abuse and told me I had to heal my childhood wounds I was shocked. How could she know this? I had never told anyone. Only certain family members suspected—I had never admitted it, even to them.

She said simply *Tonya, you need to go back there, back to what hurt you.* I said *I couldn't. It wasn't an issue any more.* I was still trying to deny and avoid. While there were other things in that reading, much of which also made sense to my life, like the heaviness I felt in my legs, feeling of being unable to move forward, the throat chakra too open blaring but not saying anything important and maybe the most profound one was the detailed image and description of me inside a castle, in the turret, hiding behind walls, wearing armor with a war waging outside the castle walls and me, trying to figure it out in my head, trying to find a logical solution to that which contained no logic.

My brain broke. I didn't understand how she could know this and yet she did. And suddenly the tears began flowing. They poured out of me with heaving sobs.

I couldn't do this. I didn't want to remember. I didn't want to go there. I couldn't go there, I wasn't strong enough. I was *fine*. I had found a way to be ok, to be able to live, to be normal, even successful. I didn't want this to be a thing.

She was very clear that this was the only thing that mattered and if I wanted to be well again and truly find myself I had to go into this, I had to deal with it, I had to heal it. But I just couldn't. I couldn't do this. I wasn't cut out for this. I wasn't strong enough for that. I couldn't face it. It was too much. I wasn't brave. I didn't want to see it, to feel it, to touch it, to know it intimately. Somehow, I felt denying it and keeping it in that box was keeping it from me.

I prayed so hard then to make all of this go away. I wanted to rewind to that exploding protein shake 2 years before and pretend it was all fine, just like any other day and never go to that workshop and never look deeper. I wished I had stayed on the surface and kept busy and never looked under the hood.

Nothing good had come from pulling back the layers and now I just felt like a broken mess of a girl who didn't know where to turn. So again, I turned away.

My night terrors returned. I have always been a vivid dreamer but these were terrors. I had them as a child, screaming, sweating, horrible, being chased nightmares, seeing the old hag, frozen in place, weights on my chest, dying inside as I was riddled with horror.

I became scared to sleep. I wasn't eating, I wasn't exercising, I wasn't going out, I was withdrawing, I was hurting and I wanted the pain to go away. I couldn't tell anyone. On the outside, it seemed like I had it together.

I had asked the question a of what had caused my eating disorders and here I was, seeing that stress and feeling out of control was causing it. I didn't have any other coping tool. Any time my life felt out of control and I needed a coping tool, I did the only thing I knew how to do to stop feeling. The pain took away the feelings but it wasn't even doing that anymore, for me.

I was turning into a very dark person. Just a few months before I was excited about life and now I was in the pits of hell. I guess there is a truth to "be careful what you ask for".

All of the things—my abuse, my feelings of never being good enough, rejected, my always being last, never anyone's first choice, not even my own—were surfacing and there was no way I could stuff down.

There was so much stuff in that black hole, so much stuff I couldn't breathe under the weight of it.

I just wanted it all to go away. I hired a coach to help me through it. I didn't care what I had to do, I had to get my life back, had to get control back. I couldn't handle this anymore. I began fantasizing about dying. Maybe if I didn't exist it would be better.

This wasn't the first time I had thoughts about dying. There was the day of the exploding protein shake, of course, but I had also been obsessed with dying as a teenager. I wanted to end it all. I never felt cared about or important to anyone. I felt like if I died no one would even notice I was gone. I had full blown eating disorders by the age of 16, was self-harming and I can't count how many times I tried to get the courage to step in front of a car, so it didn't look like I had done it myself, so no one would know.

I started talking about my abuse with my coach. In hindsight, I should have worked in an environment with sexual abuse or trauma specialists. I didn't because therapy felt different than coaching and I had done therapy for years and it hadn't helped.

As this time, I didn't realize it *was* trauma. I didn't understand trauma. I didn't understand PTSD or the effects of sexual abuse on a person. I didn't know that PTSD is something a sexual abuse survivor got. Like most people, I assumed trauma was what police officers and war vets got. I also didn't understand anxiety or depression or what it meant to be high functioning in those.

And since I didn't really feel anything I would never said I had those problems, because I thought it was people who were sad or couldn't leave their houses that had those problems. I didn't know that NOT feeling was also a problem, in fact, I believed it was a smashing success. Not even kidding.

But now I do understand. And if you are experiencing trauma, be sure you work with people who understand trauma. There are many environments and people to work with. From holistic to modern, from wisdom keepers and healers to regular therapy. It is not my place to tell you what therapies to choose, I can only share my own experiences, and what lessons I learned. And one important lesson I learned was to ensure that you're in a safe environment with someone who understands this trauma and can guide and help you properly. When we work with people who are unhealed themselves or cannot properly guide you in your recovery, it can do more damage.

Working with a coach at this time, helped me talk about, to make it real. To say, *this happened to me*. I started telling friends. Most of them were compassionate, empathetic. I was scared that I would be pitied, that was the one thing I was terrified of. But most of my friends just didn't understand why I never trusted them to share. Mostly, they didn't say anything. And it was ok, I didn't need them to say anything.

I think that was the most powerful thing that I took from it. I didn't need them to make it better, say anything or do anything. I just needed them to not look away from it and I need to get it out of me, to say to my closest people *"this is me"*. I was sorry I hadn't been there, that I couldn't open to them, that they didn't really know me. I showed them my scars and they didn't look away.

Not my closest anyway.

I had already told my husband—I did this after receiving news about my abuser's death. I didn't have to tell him then, but I did. I cringe at how cold, indifferent I was. It was matter of fact. *My abuser died. I am going to his funeral. I don't need you to come.* There was a reality at that time in our relationship that he wouldn't have come, anyway. He didn't do the uncomfortable stuff with me and I didn't ask him to. I took it all on, carried it on my own, like I had been doing my whole life. Maybe he didn't do the uncomfortable stuff because I didn't ask and in fact, said I didn't want him to. That's the truth, too. I was uncomfortable with everything and it easier if I just did it all on my own.

I never asked people to show up for me because I didn't think they would. And if I didn't ask them to and they didn't offer, then I wouldn't have to know they didn't choose me or couldn't show up for me.

It was the easy way out in some ways. I asked people not to choose me to save myself the pain when they didn't choose me.

The call was the first crack.

Things had started falling apart then but I didn't notice. I didn't notice a lot of things that year he died. It was only years after that I could connect those dots, that I realized that was the start of the breakdown, when I couldn't cope, when I started smoking, when the problems in the business and home seemed more than I could handle.

Now, two years after the exploding shake, words were slipping out of my mouth that I couldn't seem to control. I began telling people all sorts of things—things I would never ever have spoken about, things I had locked away for so long, it was like I unlocked a door that I couldn't close, oversharing and overwhelmed. It was spilling out of me.

Chapter Eight

TELL

Then, a message came for me from Mo-Mondays St. John's, could I speak in a few hours at an event as they had a cancellation and I was suggested by someone as a possible speaker. I had not spoken about my story publicly but had some public speaking experience from my fitness and health background from events and workshops I had delivered, warm ups for events and even corporate speaking gigs to talk about health and wellness.

Part of me didn't want to go. I didn't think I could do it, I was scared because this was the exact place that I had the vision of me speaking about my abuse. Part of me was screaming no but I felt as if something else was taking over my fingers as I typed the message *"thank you, I'd love to come"*.

I felt like something else was pushing me forward, like something had me in its grip and I was powerless. I was fighting inside but outside I was saying all sorts of things I wanted to run from. Inside I was telling myself to shut up. I wrote a beautiful speech that had nothing to do with my abuse.

But this place that asked me to speak? That was my vision from just a few months before on that run.

I was going to prove this "vision" and these "psychics" and "healers" wrong about all of this. Paper in hand, I was confident I could speak about anything other than my abuse. As I took the stage I felt something else take over. I began speaking without notes and that had nothing to do with the speech I had written and before I knew it I was telling an audience of more than 100 people that I had been sexually abused.

I stood there, gripped in shame and fear and overwhelm. I couldn't believe what had just happened. I stood an uncomfortably long time with the silence hanging in the air as my left brain was trying to control my mouth. But the silence dragged on so long that I couldn't find anything else to say that would be big enough to warrant the terrified pause and for the first time in my life I let myself say what was there, what was in the space.

For the first time, I didn't stuff it down, didn't make it nice, didn't make it pretty, didn't make it go away. I let it hang there, in the air. The truth. I am a survivor of childhood sexual abuse. This is what a survivor looks like. Me. Here are my wounds, my scars, my imperfections, my secrets that I hid for fear of what it would mean about it and how it would impact how people saw me, what opportunities I had and worse, what people thought of my family and worst, the abject fear of pity.

I had a standing ovation and I wanted to die. I didn't understand why I was getting a standing ovation. I didn't want to have said what I just said. I wanted to take it back. But it was out there now, all of these people, some I knew and had known a lifetime and others I had never met. I was exposed, raw, vulnerable in a way I had never allowed myself to be. And while I felt like 1000lbs had been lifted from my shoulders, I had felt deep uncertainty about what it meant for my life. I had never not controlled that story and here it was, outside of me.

I couldn't believe this had happened. It played out exactly like I had seen it play out that day on my run. I didn't like feeling like I could choose, like I had no say in what was happening in my life anymore.

I didn't recognize myself. I didn't know who I was becoming and I wasn't sure I liked this messy out of control person I was. I liked to make things happen, to be in control, to control the story, what people knew.

That ship had, clearly, sailed.

Chapter Nine

JAGUAR

Over the next year I felt stagnant at times and better at other times. I was on a rollercoaster where I just wanted to get better. I didn't like feeling this way. I was dark, brooding, overwhelmed, frustrated, angry and annoyed at everything. Life was heavy. I was seeing a lot of problems with everyone and everything.

Soon I stopped fighting it. I just sank into it. I wasn't getting better, I was getting worse. I stopped showering. I stopped working out. I was angry. All the time. I didn't get out of bed and I felt like I weighed 1000lbs, the weight of the world was on top of me as I replayed moments from my life over and over again while simultaneously trying to get back to the girl I used to know, the girl who was full of piss and vinegar, who was so hopeful and excited and who didn't give a crap about anything.

How had this been better? How had unpacking and looking and finding and uncovering WHY been better than what I was living before? I wanted my off button. I wanted to not feel and get back to living.

My friends were worried. My husband was seeing an ugly side of me. Everyone thought I had walked off the deep end. And I had. This was not the surface. I was out to sea without a compass, without a boat and no paddles. I was floating and directionless, lost.

None of the tools I had been learning were working. Meditation, prayer, mindset, and thinking positive—it all just made me feel like a bigger failure. And I was mad about that too—2 years and dozens of courses, programs and 3 coaches and I couldn't get out of bed, I wasn't showering, and I was dreaming of death.

I was lying in a sea of nothingness and I felt stupid. Why had I even started down this path?

One morning, something snapped inside of me. I felt myself fading away as I stared at the ceiling. Without my dogs I wasn't sure I'd still be here. I knew they needed me and they loved me. So, I got up to walk them. I fed them. I cuddled with them. I played with them. They kept me going. One snuggled me and one made me move. They were my fearless leaders, my guides, my grounding, my protectors far more than I could ever be theirs.

They gave me far more in this lifetime than I have ever given them.

That morning I knew I needed help. I knew if I didn't get it I wouldn't be here soon. I couldn't feel like this anymore. It had been a year since Las Vegas and despite meditation classes, retreats, positive thinking and coaches I was feeling worse than I had ever felt in my life.

I didn't know it at the time but the wild was calling me. A battle cry had been sent out. My soul was desperate to live, to breathe. A part of me that had been lost, buried under that baggage, was clawing her way back into my life. I couldn't move forward in my life without clearing that black hole. And as long as I resisted it, I would be here, in this space of nothing, forever.

What was left to do? I had done it all I thought. So, I prayed. I still didn't know if I believed in God but I didn't know what else to do. I needed help and I didn't know where else to go.

Suddenly I was reminded of a woman I had met at a meditation group I had attended. She had not been there before.

I sat next to her but felt I had to move and crossed the room to sit directly across from her. As we meditated, I was, once again, not there, not in the room, not thinking, not visualizing like I did in most meditations... I was somewhere else.

I was in a field, I recognized it as somewhere I had been before but I had not, in my real life, been there. The grass was long, taller than me but I wasn't afraid. I was floating almost in the stillness of the field as my fingertips brushed across the grass. In this place I could smell it, taste it and feel it all as though it were real.

I had no realization of my body back on a sofa in the meditation room. This was my reality. And just as real was the snarling massive black jaguar that appeared in front of me. He was frothing from the mouth, dripping drool, foam covering his face. Yet, I wasn't scared. I knew him. I had met him before, somehow, but again I had not actually known him, but my soul did.

I reached out to pet him and he let me, although he was still snarling, as if to impart a message that I didn't understand. We fell into step together, walking comfortably in silence. I felt safe, protected, and very intense. He rolled on his back, playing and I was laughing like a little girl.

We were called back to the room but I didn't want to leave. I wanted to stay there with him. I had never felt this kind of peace in my life. And especially after the last year, I needed peace.

But as quickly as I had gone, I was back staring at this woman across from me. As we shared our experience with the group, I asked if anyone knew the significance of a jaguar, it was common for my fellow meditators to have animal experiences but I had not had one until now. This woman was excited as she shared some tidbits with me—seer of the dark, helps us find and mulch up things, a powerful spirit animal.

That experience had been months ago. And while I enjoyed the jaguar experience I wondered if I should see my regular doctor for medications at this point. Or even perhaps to admit how badly I was feeling and check myself into a hospital. Perhaps trying to heal more naturally wasn't helping. In fact, most things seemed to only make me worse.

But the pull to her was strong, it wouldn't go away. Something made me reach out to her. I was scared, nervous, hesitant, yet I went to see her. I told her I had been feeling very low. I wasn't in a good place and I needed some help but I didn't know what I needed.

I went to her home and a healing room inside of her home. I took the chair opposite her. I didn't know what to do. There were drawings on the wall, crystals, a massage bed, rattles, bottles of stuff, paintings. I was weary but I was there.

I told her so much that day about how I had been really feeling. I told her that I had reached out to 2 friends and told them I was suffering and struggling and they basically told me I loved the struggle and to get over it or to think positive.

I was scared. I had only started dealing with my abuse less than a year before. I felt there was no grace, no support. In the space where I helped so many people in their bad days, I didn't feel it was returned to me and I was angry. I was so angry. It all spilled over and out and I was angry at everyone. I cried rivers of tears, shed mountains of anger, told her things I had never told anyone else, it all just came pouring out. I told her how I was really feeling. I was there for hours with everything spilling out of me. Exhausted, I sat down, feeling spent, but free in some strange way to be allowed to say and feel what I felt.

I wasn't told I was wrong. I was just allowed to let it out. I was ready to go home.

Regina handed me a rattle and began drumming. *Let's get started* she said.

Mouth gaping, reeling, wondering how I had gotten into this, I stood stock still as she opened sacred space, had me blow my issues into a rock, checked my chakra's and took me through a release of the things I had just told her.

I was uncertain of what was happening, what I felt and what I thought of this. I didn't want to offend her but I was certain I was completely nuts at this point.

I didn't go gracefully into this world of spirit or healing or holistic work or shamanic work. I left claw marks on the door. My mind wandered, would people think this is crazy? Is this crazy? Am I crazy? Maybe this is it…this is the end of it all for me.

Yet, leaving, I felt better. I felt safe. I felt heard. I felt validated. I felt like all the things that I been feeling and experiencing I was given permission to feel. I took the mask off and the air on my face felt so good.

I began to feel better. For the first time in a long time I felt peace, calm and I felt something else I couldn't quite put my finger on. She explained spirit animals and jaguar medicine to me. Told me to call on him to help me find and release more of the toxic stuff inside of me.

"Like files on a computer, an imprint is left behind in us when things don't pass through us, when they are stored. The ancient medicine men and women have known for centuries that our light body holds onto experiences that impact our life force, our energy, it can shut down one or more, even all, of chakra's—the body's energy centers.

Deleting the imprints that are in the light body will rebalance your energy and remove its impact in your life. Not just the abuse, but anything that you're still holding onto".

It made sense, now, that what I had been through, the conditioning, my abuse, the living a life of should, the inability to stand up for myself, the doormat, all of that was coming up for me and I was trying to stuff it all back in. But stuffing it down, changing its meaning, changing my perception of it wasn't helping because the imprint was stuck in my light body.

"You are called for a bigger purpose. This is your dark night of the soul" she said.

I could no longer pretend or band aid things. I had to go into these things, to let myself feel what I felt that I had never allowed myself to feel. She explained that my light energy field was holding onto this stuff, stored inside of me.

I was in my own dark night of the soul. This darkness that weighs our soul down must be explored and cleansed. It must be felt, every single piece of it. It was ok to surrender to the pain. I didn't need to pretend here.

This is not a passing sadness. The dark night of the soul is the pain that occurs when our soul has experienced something painful. A wound to our soul unhealed will eventually turn up in behaviors in our lives. I didn't know my soul could be wounded. I don't know if I actually knew I had a soul at this point. I didn't know someone could experience soul loss. But when we are compromised and cannot express it or heal it, it gets stuffed down inside of us and turns toxic, impacting our energy centers in the body—Our chakra's.

I had stirred up so much stuff over the last year but I had nothing to *do* with it. No one I had worked with had given me the tools to do anything with this stuff that was coming up for me, so I pushed it all down again. But it wouldn't stay down there anymore. And most people were just asking me to shake it off but I didn't know how.

Like a jack in box, my bits and pieces were all over the floor, everything I had stored was out there for me to see and feel and I had to work through it in order to restore balance to my life.

I had never learned to work through anything. I didn't understand or know my emotions. I had only known denial and avoidance.

The dark night of the soul was calling me to explore the darkness. It was asking me to break it all down and let my pain lead me through. It went against what I learned. Everything I had been learning was about changing how I thought and felt about it. So, this didn't make sense. Now, I was asking it to rise? To bubble up to the surface, bring me more of it?

Reframing and repatterning are great when you've processed your emotions but not before. I began to study emotions, to learn about the energy centers in our body and what happens when we don't deal with things, when we avoid pain.

Positive thinking was helping me pretend. I had been pretending my entire life. Now in order to truly heal I had to let it up. I had to explore it, I had to experience what I refused to experience when it happened.

Chapter Ten

DARK

I was being called to release the emotions and the experiences so the past wasn't pulling me back into them, causing me to create the same experiences over and over again because the lessons weren't learned, the growth hadn't happened because I refused to deal with them. The experiences were still trapped in my body.

It's not only our mind that holds onto things. Our body does as well. Our cells, like trauma passed on from our family or society, hold the experiences we've had and unless we do something to move those experiences, they will stay stuck in us and keep drawing us back into the same things that these unhealed experiences and emotions are calling to teach us.

The call of the wild had been sent out. A year earlier I was shown the darkness, the stuff that had to be released, but I was still trying to skip over it, trying to ignore the big issues. Still not really allowing myself to feel or heal.

I asked some very profound questions—why are we the way we are. Why do we repeat the cycles over and over again? I had asked why I had eating disorders, why did all these things keep happening. Now I was being shown the reasons. When we ask questions, we'll get answers. I was being led to my answers. I didn't like them but I was being shown why we keep repeating cycles and patterns and habits.

I could no longer learn and teach from the mind. I was being shown my soul connection and if I was doing the work I was born to do I had to take this journey. The work I was doing was only a small part of what I was meant to do and if I was truly going to step into the role—to get the "click" that I was waiting for, I had to do this.

I didn't know at the time that my work would change. I was just trying to heal myself so I could focus on work again. I wasn't here to do the surface or easy work. I was here to go deep into that darkness.

The dark night of the soul gives rise to extraordinary work. When we go beyond the symptoms and the surface and allow ourselves to lean into and allow the pain to be our greatest teacher, what has the potential to rise from this is extraordinary.

Many of the greatest teachers on the earth had experienced their own dark night of the soul—the deepest and darkest stuff that we can experience.

I was here to unmask myself, to let it all be there, seeing it for what it was, not what I wanted it to be. I had been about to embark on the wrong plan, the wrong journey, again. But this time the universe put some hard blocks in my place. It refused to let me go that route, it was drawing me to where it was time to go.

Denying my story meant I denied the things that made me resilient, denied access to my power now it was time to own my story and how it shaped my life.

Going into the dark is scary. We aren't sure what will happen. And most people are certainty and significance driven. We don't know how it will go, so we don't go in. We aren't sure of the outcome and people who love certainty above all else will keep finding ways to not do the deeper work. They will find ways to keep pretending.

And in my case, I was scared that I wouldn't be ok if I went in there. What would happen if I couldn't cope? If I became more broken? What if I got into the eye of the storm and couldn't handle it?

I wasn't certainty driven at this point in my life. I was driven by something deeper that was calling to me and I was being driven more by variety than anything else—making this journey possible because even though I was scared it was far better than not feeling at all.

I was scared. I didn't know if I believed in this but something inside of me was awakening and opening up, drifting, clearing, clawing. Something that seemed to remember. Something intriguing. But mostly, I felt safe. I felt that I wasn't crazy or a drama queen. I felt like I was being nurtured and loved for the first time in my life.

In fact, it was on my shamans, my medicine woman's massage table one day that I felt unconditional love for the first time. So, I kept going. For the first time in my life I felt like I belonged somewhere, I didn't feel judged or condemned or wrong.

She directed me to open a sand painting—she warned me I would feel worse before I felt better. A sand painting is a circle opened for the intention of finding hidden things inside of us—asking the stuck emotions to rise up, giving it a space to open and using the earth elements to help us.

I opened it on a private part of my property. My husband knew I was working on mindset and had coaches but he had no idea what I was into really. And I was scared he would think I had lost my mind if he knew. As it turned out, when I let him in, he cut the wood for my fires and showed me the best trees on the property.

But at this time, I had no idea what I was doing myself and didn't know how to explain it. I was also very angry with him and couldn't share much with him because my anger was keeping him at bay. I was pushing him away all the time.

Using sticks and pieces of things from nature I was to create a circle and using sticks, rocks, leaves and stones, anything I could find, I would "blow the issues or problems" I was experiencing or the emotions I was feeling or the triggers I was dealing with into pieces of outside debris. Once the issue was blown into the piece, it is laid into the circle, where it gains energy and grows, opening a portal of sorts to deeper issues. Like peeling back an onion, layer by layer.

Once opened (the sand painting is considered opened once it's created and issues are blown into it) as I felt things I would blow my emotions into sticks and rocks and place them in the center, allowing it to grow in energy as well as having somewhere to actually release it. My shaman had prepared me that this would be emotional, even painful as experiences and memories beyond the ones I had been playing on repeat would begin to come up—as layers of emotions were released, deeper ones would come.

With each piece I released I took a deep breath and blew what I was feeling, rage, confusion, sadness, anger, overwhelm, not enough and at that time there was a lot of processing of people in my life—relationships with friends, family were being blown into this circle, to process.

The black hole was finally getting the attention it was calling for. And it reared up far more powerfully than I could have prepared myself for. I called my shaman, hysterical after 2 days. I had felt so good when I left her place. Why was this happening? I couldn't handle these intense feelings of anger and sadness mixed together, the inability to push it down and move on. They were too intense. I felt like I was being torn into bits. I had been a master at being unemotional and in control of my emotions, this was new territory and I wasn't sure I was ever going to get over this.

She took me through a similar session via distance to help me release these intense and painful memories and emotions. She reassured me this was normal, that they were many layers to be healed, so much stuff I had ignored and had festering and turned malignant.

Talking about them is one thing but truly releasing them, choosing to heal them was another part. I didn't realize how much stuff was buried in that black hole. The good feelings were short lived as more and more negative ones surfaced. And the anger, it was explosive, volatile, and not anything I had ever allowed myself to experience.

With the anger, I had the mixed emotions of guilt and shame for feeling how I felt. Things I had told myself at the time were unimportant. I explained them away but they were still there, clearly, I had wanted or wished for or hoped for something different but I never asked for it, I just said "ok". And these were stuck to other events and people in my life where I had also felt these things, where family, parents, and friends didn't choose me or show up for me. I had so many unanswered questions, unprocessed emotions that now were coming up.

It was like a ball of yarn, everything connected to things it shouldn't be connected to and unravelling it was like pulling apart a giant mess and trying to make sense of what meant what, what was connected and what wasn't.

I made it easy for others not to choose me. I never asked for what I *really* wanted.

I didn't ask him to choose me or make me important. I didn't ask for help, I didn't ask him to be there for me. Perhaps in some childlike way I had hoped he would be there for me but he wasn't. It was only now I could see my own active part in it. I told him not to him come... because then it would be my decision and not his. I would be the one standing alone, being independent and not being rejected, not being made unimportant, not being overlooked.

But it was all there, every time he wasn't there for me, even though I told him not to be. It festered and bubbled like a raging pot. I couldn't control it. I wanted to smash him and us and me and make it all stop hurting.

Later I would realize the real perspective—often we push people away, they go, then we blame them for going, we're inflicting pain on them, too, that we can't see because we're so caught in our own pain. I couldn't see what it was like to be in a relationship with someone who never ever opened, who constantly pushed you away and acted like she didn't care.

Chapter Eleven

SILENCE

I wasn't at rock bottom; I was in rock bottom's basement. I was clearing out the trenches of sludge that had been impacted inside of me, stuck in my energy field. I wasn't consciously holding onto it, but subconsciously I was hanging on so tight my knuckles were white. It was like holding onto the knife by the blade. I said one thing, wanted another and then stored it and looked away from it but it was still there.

Piece after piece, up it came, all attached to hundreds of other experiences where I felt rejected, misunderstood, unimportant, unseen. A child who had decided a long time ago to get off the path, to not need anyone and to push them away before they could push me away.

My family life growing up was chaotic, to put it mildly. I was a sensitive child. I liked to play and write stories. I had a vivid and wild imagination. I loved to draw and color and I was fairly reserved. With 5 kids and growing up the middle child, I often felt like I was trying to make things better for everyone. It was like I knew what people wanted and I tried to give it to them. I was an enabler and didn't know it.

I felt bad. For everything and everyone. I felt like a disappointment and disappointed my whole life. I always felt unseen, unheard, unimportant. I struggled deeply with my feelings and began to check out at an early age.

I felt I shouldn't think bad things about my parents or my family, because I also knew that they had done the best they could. But another part of me wanted to justify it and explain it away. I always wanted to justify and explain away people's reasons for not being there for me. I don't know why I did that, why I made it easy for people not to choose me or why I just couldn't face the truth, I didn't want to be a bother or a burden or add anything extra to people.

But I also just liked to pretend that things were better than they were. So being in this place of feeling like a victim, being dark, negative, angry was a different place for me.

I also felt like a burden. It was a mess to experience. I couldn't help the hurt of a child and I couldn't help making it all mean what I did. Now it was coming up and I was feeling guilty for what I had felt as a child. It was a vicious circle.

The more I stirred up in sessions and sand paintings and writing, calling on spirit animals and the spirit world, the extraordinary, and the things long forgotten and unprocessed, the further I fell and I stopped trying to get up. I let my knees hit the floor as the pain of a lifetime washed over me. I let myself be broken, messy and hurt. I let myself feel, for the first time in my life. I didn't turn away from it. And it was hard. It was hard to look at it all, to see how little I had asked for, how little I accepted and how much I had ignored.

It was hard to see that I made myself small, that I shrunk myself and made it easy for no one to choose me. In fact, I insisted that to make their life easier I would just remove myself from the equation.

Consciously I ignored it but my body stored it. It was there and it was impacting me whether I realized it or not. I had turned away from life, from living, from love and connection. I made the choice to stop caring. I remember being so hurt one day that I decided I didn't need anyone else and I turned away, turned my back on who I was, who I used to be, I threw away all of my caring and my softness that made me weak. I developed a hard shell. I became someone who just didn't care and couldn't be hurt.

This person was in control of my life. Not the real me, but the person I became because I was tired of feeling that way, tired of being hurt, tired of caring. I was making decisions from this space, which impacted my business and my life.

I let myself express it, say it, write it, and let it out. I let myself not need to be somewhere else. I accepted that this needed to done, that it was ok to feel all that I never allowed myself to feel. I stopped pretending it was fine, that I was fine. I wasn't fine. None of this was fine. The more I cleared the more came up.

Would there ever be an end to this? How much was in there? Everything tied together in one big knot—who I had become—whatever they wanted me to be. I had lost myself and to hide the scars, the wounds I carried I just did and became in everything situation what I thought I was supposed to.

I had turned away from people but my inherent human need for love and support was still there and I had to find ways to meet that need. I didn't believe it was available so I would go inside and get it in a make-believe world.

On the outside I nodded and smiled, I kept the peace, but in my mind, I was in this other space. I didn't need to get my needs met outside of me, I was getting them met in a fantasy world. I knew this wasn't real, but it didn't stop me from doing it.

It started as a child to get away from my reality. Then it continued on anytime I needed to escape from reality. I never dealt with anything because I just slipped away when things got uncomfortable.

I recalled dinners where my grandmother talked about my abuser, her son, my father's brother and visiting him in the mental hospital. He was remanded to custody because he wasn't mentally fit for prison. I wanted to scream and tell her to shut up, that no one cared about him and I wanted to know why she always chooses him and not us? As an adult, I can understand that he was her child, but as a child I just wanted to scream.

But instead I ate in silence and waited for her to finish. My parents raised polite children. We weren't allowed to speak back. We had to be polite, especially to people older than us. So I swallowed it down.

Becoming a harder version of myself was my way of escaping. I didn't have to be the good girl. I was snarky, passive aggressive; I was dark and brooding and didn't care. I emerged the darkened butterfly, the black nail polish, the smoking, the not eating girl, the girl with edges so sharp I cut you if you came within feet of me.

It's no wonder that I couldn't find my voice to speak up, to ask for what I wanted, instead I always waited for someone else to say it, to give it to me, to tell me.

As I uncovered more of these experiences I realized how many times I had been silenced. How many times my voice was taken from me and how often I silenced myself. The truth was rising in so many ways that I wanted to deny. It became a memory I couldn't repress that my grandmother knew of the abuse. I pushed this into recesses of the black hole, the box of darkness because it was easier than facing the truth of it.

My attitude, my behaviors surfaced as a way to say something. Instead of saying what I wanted to, instead of asking the questions I wanted to ask, I was snarky, rude, disrespectful, and angry.

Memories began to surface. Like the day my grandmother whispered in my ear to not go to her house when she wasn't home. I had forgotten this memory along with 3 other experiences where it was clear that she knew, but she ignored it.

As my rage and heartache and despair engulfed me I felt that little girl who could see people choosing to look away. I could feel what it felt like to be ignored. No wonder I felt unimportant. No wonder I shut down. I felt shame too. Shame that he was more important than me. How worthless and unimportant was I that she chose him?

When the police came I refused to tell. I was scared when I first saw the police car when I got off the school bus. I was questioned by my mother and another relative and threatened with the police. I thought I was in trouble because the police weren't something we were taught to help us. In fact, they were used as fear tactics to get us to behave or they'd call the police. Now I was in front of them and scared out of my mind so I zipped my lips, swearing to myself I'd never let anyone know.

I will never forget that day, standing in the bedroom my sister and I shared, my mother and other relative on the bottom bunk of the bunk beds we shared. The bedspread was pink lace and I couldn't breathe in the too small for all of us room. My school bag hanging in my right hand, a memory etched in time for me.

While I had been abused for nearly a decade, no one knew but this was the day, the very moment, that a part of me was lost, locked away, left to wither as I desperately fought the truth.

The kids on the bus made horrible rhymes up about my family because they were cruel. We were terrorized and bullied by the other kids. Songs were made up and friends distanced themselves from us. I chose to save myself. I refused to be "one of the abused" so I lied. I lied and I lied and I lied until everyone left me alone.

And eventually they did. And I was alone. Inside of myself. I shoved myself into that cage and threw away the key. I became someone no one could hurt. I was 9, I think. By the age of 11 or 12 the court case was happening and everyone else involved was called to testify to the abuse they suffered at his hands. But I checked out. I walked away. It was too much for me. I just wanted to be normal.

It's only been in conversations these last few years that I understand what it was like for them, what they endured, their experience and how different it was from mine. Same trauma, different outcomes, different residual trauma from silencing ourselves or speaking the truth.

It was during my healing journey that I learned who told and how that day unfolded. My mother and grandmother were walking from the store when the police stopped them and asked to bring her home, they wanted to talk to her. My mother would soon find out that her daughters were being sexually abused, and were waiting for us when we got off the school bus.

Looking back now as a woman who has healed her deepest wounds, I often feel intense compassion and empathy for my mother, having to experience that, having to hear that, having to know, believe and try to do something with that, she was the one who kept us updated on the trial, over the years it was her who told us of parole hearings, need-to-know information and it was her who protected my story right until I chose to share it.

I didn't want to be *that* girl. I just wanted to be normal, to fit in, to be accepted and liked and a part of something.

One day after school I went to play with my sister and others involved. They had been in court that day. And I wasn't. So, they rejected me. As an adult I can understand, but as a child, I just left, withering further inside of me. Earlier that week my childhood friends had played another cruel joke on me, making it clear they didn't want me to be around. I had become the brunt of their schemes and bullying.

Another moment of impact, etched in the light field, burned in my memory and another bar in the cage around my heart as they faked a pen pal for me with the intention of setting me up to be made fun of.

One girl was nice enough to tell me the truth about the pen pal, among other schemes they were cooking up to embarrass and humiliate me. I was getting good at running away and shrinking into myself in shame by the time I was 13.

I made decisions then, not just little decisions, but soul decisions, soul contracts, that I would never ever be open to people that way again, never ever allow anyone to get close enough to hurt me.

I had forgotten all of this in my conscious mind, shoved down into the box with all the other things, but there it was, in that black hole, more proof that I wasn't good enough, that I was someone no one wanted.

The pain was unbearable. I wanted it to stop. I kept asking if this was normal, that what good was there in remembering this pain? There was a reason I stuffed it away. Why did this matter, it all seemed so childish? Why did I need to relive this? My shaman always reminded me that this was there, inside of me, and pretending it wasn't, wasn't going to help me. It was going to keep me half living. It was going to hold me back from fulfilling my purpose and when the dark night of the soul was over it would make sense. Something would be revealed to me.

I had so much disdain inside of me that I didn't know was there. I just couldn't understand why people would be so cruel. How could you look away from a child knowing she was being abused? How could children be so cruel to each other? How could life go so wrong?

Why in all of this did I decide it was something wrong with me? So in a cruel world, I closed. Closed my heart. Stepped out of my body. And became someone different.

I didn't want that story, so I decided to create a new one. I decided to become the girl who didn't care, who didn't need anyone and who expected to be screwed over by people and I just wouldn't let it bother me.

The black hole was teaching me why I had become the person I did. It was showing me all the things that had led to living the life I was. I had asked for this journey. It was showing me the things that had happened that I had written off, pushed away but that were there, the bricks formed the walls I hide behind and the stones became the spikes in the suit I wore. They were the rungs in the massive gates and the crocodiles in the moat.

PART 3

PROCESSING

Becoming who we are is the privilege of a lifetime.

Chapter Twelve

STIR

The more that came up the lower I sank. I clung to the concept that it would get better if I would just let it up. So I kept finding ways to let it up, pen to paper, I stirred the pot. I rattled, I shook, I meditated, I prayed, I called on the jaguar, I walked, I hiked, I cried, I wailed, I screamed, I wrote until my hands cramped and bled, I burned.

I burned it all down. Bridges. Relationships. Things. Businesses. I spoke. I cut. I told where I was, unapologetically me. I had been burned, torn down, ripped apart and I was still standing—bruised and battered but I was still here. I knew I was making people uncomfortable. A lot of people left me.

And I didn't care. I couldn't care. I was tired of caring more about other people's feelings, placating, silencing, stuffing it down, playing nice and being pleasing at a cost of the truth. I was tired of not asking to be treated better or for what was mine.

I was just tired of holding it all in and while it was ugly I wouldn't do it any differently because it was a purge of all that was ugly. I was finding my voice, my footing, myself in a new world.

I let it all up—everything that was ready to come up and there was so much of it. My first boyfriend who wanted to fool around but didn't want anyone to know; he told me it was more special when no one else was involved or could influence us. By then I was used to keeping secrets, what was wrong with this one?

And then I found out he was publicly dating my friend. We were 13. How is it that a 13-year-old boy even knows how to pull that stuff off?

The 34-year-old dude who used me when I was 15. He should be in jail, really. What IS wrong with a 34-year-old man who seduces and manipulates a 15-year-old girl? I know what was wrong with me. I was looking for love in all the wrong places. But him?

I always thought there was something wrong with me. It seemed like I pushed away the good things and settled into the bad things. Slice after slice the memories, the realizations, the rose-colored glasses removed to see how it really was. And it was ugly, the memories, the lack of self-respect, the other kind of wild, girls gone wild, don't care girl.

I had painted myself a far better picture than it was. And in fact, I'm not sure there was a picture at all most of the time. I had little to no memories of my childhood. I struggled to remember details, years, people, times and places. Actually, I had almost no memories of my life in general. At this time in my journey I had huge gaps, even years that seemed to be missing.

I think I didn't like who I was, who I had become. How I behaved. What I did and didn't do so I just turned them off.

I met this guy who, it turns out, I had hooked up with in university. I hadn't been drunk, but I couldn't remember him. I had no idea who he was. He remembered me, my name, even where I lived. I had no recollection of him. At all. I wasn't really there. There were so many of these memories surfacing that it was crippling me.

The situations I barely got out of with my life and what I did to get out of those situations made me cringe, vomiting rising more than once as I remembered how little respect I had for myself to end up there in the first place. And the intense knowing that it was put out and pretend or it would end far worse for me.

There is something that dies inside of you when you choose to pretend and give in, acting like you like it, blaming yourself for it and washing it off the next day as you numb yourself to the memories then laugh it off with your friends later. And do it all another weekend... pulling the truth up was harrowing. I wished it would all stay down into the abyss where I had put it.

My body and my subconscious processed these things while I checked out, looked the other way and avoided. I was not consciously in control of my life. The results I had in life were directly because I refused to deal with anything. I never actually said no, I never said anything but I vented about it all, complained about it in any way I could. I would release the charge by talking about it and not actually doing anything to change it and I couldn't speak to the people about and I certainly never talked about it anyone who mattered or asked to be treated differently

I used to ask, "how could they?" It wasn't just in life, it showed up in business too. People cancelled, stole from me, spread rumors about me, bounced checks, cancelled their payments. I had a lawyer tell me she would call and report me for something and even though it wasn't true, it would be enough to destroy me because by the time they fixed it I'd be out of money.

True story. I can't make this stuff up. Real life is crazier than the movies. But I never did anything about any of it. I let it go on. Never did I fight back. Why? Well, the black hole was where I shoved it all.

Chapter Thirteen

STUCK

began to see why I wasn't having the results I wanted, why things were always going wrong and why people treated me like that. I rolled out the carpet and lay down for them. I apologized they told me I wasn't flat enough to walk on and shrunk myself smaller.

It fit my belief that there was something wrong with me.

But even more interesting was that I never wanted to hurt people's feelings. Even though they didn't care about hurting mine. I guess I knew how it felt to have people say things that weren't ok. Sometimes I did snap and say things that were hurtful or mean, or passive aggressive after it had built up for long enough. Then I always felt immense shame and guilt for doing it and I'd do anything to make it better.

I never spoke up because I reminded myself of all of my own behaviors. Did I have a right to say anything? What would I say? Would people think I shouldn't have said anything? I internalized and shoved it down.

I knew I couldn't stay in this place, that if I was going to get well I had to figure out how to change this story, to turn it around. I had to find a way to understand this and heal. I had to get well. I knew I wasn't born for this to be my story.

It was time to take back my control. The purge and the dark night of the soul was important but I had to get back up. It was time.

I poured over the manuals, the trainings, the books, the coaching, the meditations, the programs and courses I had taken over the last few years, even went back to what I did to adopt a healthy mindset and healthy lifestyle years before and came up with an idea.

If I could keep releasing all of this stuff how could I forgive, really forgive, how could I understand it all and let it go?

The *untethered soul* tells us that experiences unprocessed and unhealed in our lives will create triggers. Basically, the experiences are stuck somewhere in our body, stored in our chakra's, muddying up our energy field and every time something happens that is attached to it, reminds us of it, we will be drawn into the negative energy of it.

The way through is to allow us to process the emotions. To feel it all like it was happening now. That's where I found rock bottom, feeling 34 years' worth of stuff—stuffing it down, not being seen, unimportant, abused, used, manipulated, changing myself to fit in, being someone, I wasn't to get attention, putting out, putting up with...all of it.

It's not a nice place when you see the big picture of how you've shown up. How you've let that happen, how you choose that, how you had no self-worth, no self-respect, no self-identity except to fit in, be wanted and be pleasing.

I always found a way to blame myself for everything. No matter what happened in life I would always come full circle to remind myself of how I had been or my own reactions. I took responsibility to clean up what was not mine to clean up.

I just wanted everything to be normal.

In reality things were happening but I was looking away, slipping into my mind to a place where I could pretend things were fine. And I didn't have to be uncomfortable, I didn't have to deal with anything, I didn't have to feel anything. I didn't have to change anything.

We are so conditioned to shut down, to not speak our truth, to not feel that we become shells of human beings—my grandfather used to say there's a lot of bodies with no heads walking around, disconnected.

But he also missed the no heart. We aren't IN life. We don't experience it. We are cut off and numb and the only way through that is to feel it.

You've got to feel it all. I always felt as though I were floating, not in the story. I could be at a party, an event and I always felt like I was watching the room, checking everything out but never remember being there. There were times I didn't want to be somewhere but instead of saying no I went along but I slipped away in my mind, went somewhere else.

I couldn't remember things because I wasn't there. I could remember events and details of my make belief life but not from my real world.

I was angry because of the results I had in my life but the results were a direct result of not asking for what I wanted, not being honest about what I felt about anything. I pretended the very things I wanted in life I didn't want.

It was living a nightmare instead of a dream. Justifiably jaded, acting the part, protesting and hating the things I secretly dreamed of and wanted.

The dark night of the soul, the allowing this stuff to come up was a shock to me, I couldn't believe how much stuff I couldn't see, how much stuff I was avoiding and ignoring. I had not spent my life thinking of these things. In fact, it was the total opposite

I honestly today cannot imagine living so closed, so oblivious to things as I did then. My autoresponder to life was to get angry, have a meltdown and then slip away to create a better story in my mind. It happened so quickly I didn't realize I was doing it. It's a quick figure 8… something happens, react, do something to get out of that reaction, slip away. Until the next time.

On some level I think I knew what I was doing, what I was thinking was not normal, how I was dreaming of another reality wasn't normal. But I never changed my own reality. I let things happen, let things go, didn't deal with it but painted a picture in my mind of something else, I went somewhere else into this world and met all of my needs with other characters, other jobs, other life events.

I was living 2 lives—one in my mind and one in reality.

Chapter Fourteen

SURRENDER

A ctually, talking about this, facing it, allowing it to be there in my present space was immensely shameful. Because in my fantasy world I wasn't this person. In my fantasy world I was someone who didn't walk around anything but in reality, I was a doormat who dealt with nothing and was going along with everything.

It was a painful realization. A soul shattering, shameful reality that I was pretending in my mind to be someone I wasn't, that the only person I was fooling was myself.

I surrendered.

I had no choice anymore. The pain was simply too much to bear. The fight, the swords. The walls. The shame. The rage. The weight of what I had carried and all I continued to carry, washed over me.

I couldn't fight it anymore. I didn't want to fight it anymore. I had nothing left to fight. Here I was. My scars, my wounds, my imperfections. My too much ness, my trauma, my hurt, my rage, my retaliation, my door mat, my love, my hate, my passion and blah all mixed into one place.

I screamed. I shook. I danced. I let it all out. Whatever poison was left inside of me, I wailed out, I cried, I wrote, I burned, I prayed.

The wild had come. And she wasn't going away. She was coursing through my veins, my life, my world as she surrendered me to the pain, as she held me in the embrace that only the wild within can do.

As I fell, not caring where I landed, not caring about anything but not in the depression, giving up sort of way, in the beast sort of way, in the warrior reclaimed sort of way, in the goddess gone mad sort of way.

Things had been volatile in my marriage for some time, but we were both good at pretending and looking away from what we didn't want to acknowledge. We actually didn't fight much, we were more the silent treatment type, the brooding type, but he could be explosive so I treaded carefully a lot.

I was not the same girl he married and I felt like he needed me to be someone I wasn't or at least wasn't anymore. He doesn't like change and I had turned our lives into confetti without asking or telling or even talking about it. I had become what he wanted me to be but now I wasn't playing that game and it created a space of frustration with me. He couldn't do anything right because he was doing what he had always done but what he had always done was now driving me mad.

And while we didn't talk a lot about it, there was a distance that grown between us, that distance was on and off. At times I felt closer and connected to him and other times I felt closed and frustrated. And the difference was in what I was focusing on. So many days I only focused on the stuff he didn't do right, on how we were wrong, throwing the past back in his face.

In surrendering, I couldn't pretend anymore. I had aired out so many areas of my life, so much stuff, trauma, drama, my own shadows, it was time to at least have the difficult conversation about what was in the space between us instead of pretending there was no space between us.

I found myself on my knees in front of my husband sobbing my heart, my hurt, my wounds, my lostness, my journey, my unfoldment, my containment to him. I wouldn't and couldn't go into a box, not for him, not for anyone, not anymore. I had finally found myself and wouldn't pretend to make him more comfortable, to make anyone more comfortable.

I wouldn't half live and pretend anymore. I wouldn't play the game we had been playing for so long, of wanting but not asking and hoping and wishing. While this piece is hard to write because we have both changed so much since then, it's also the truth as it was then and huge piece in my story of unbecoming what and who I wasn't… the decision that I was going to be myself, even if that meant no one, including my husband, and myself, knew who that was or what it meant for us.

And it will be difficult for this to be out there but this was a huge piece for me in healing, in seeing how I silenced myself, how I let myself be silenced, how I let him treat me, choose me or not choose me.

And then how I justified treating him in return. We cannot only see one side. If we are to become who we are really we also have to see our own shadows. And that also was that I never asked for anything different, I never spoke up, never stood up, I let it all go, then festered on it. And I wasn't there for him either. I made everything else more important because honestly, relationships and love were too scary. Now I wanted more, was ready for more.

I couldn't do it anymore, the way we had been doing things. And if he couldn't accept me for who I was, then I couldn't change that. But what I would no longer change, was me.

I am who I am. All broken pieces, sharp edges and trauma and surviving and dreaming and passionate and driven and connected all at the same time. I was the universe and the universe were me. I wouldn't stuff myself down or dull myself anymore.

I wouldn't be "that girl" he knew anymore. I was never her, I just became her, that's the only version of me he knew and she didn't live here anymore.

I would stand up for myself. I would say no. I wouldn't be pleasing or conditioned anymore. And as I lay on the floor in front of him that day I felt him see me, maybe for the first time. Maybe because I finally let enough walls down that he could *finally* see me.

There was a realness, a connection, a truth of that outpouring that was between us that hadn't been there before. And it was a beautiful space. A realness where the hurts we had done to each other, the not there for each other, the closed spaces, the turning off, the spikes, the walls… it was all gone.

It's easy for me to be caught up in what he did to me. How he was and wasn't there for me. But it was harder for me to see, also, that I wasn't there, wasn't available, and ultimately that I was the one who pretended to be someone I wasn't, the one who had walls up, pushed him away, then blamed him for going. I'm not justifying or washing the truth because there is a truth that both of us were hurting and we were hurting each other by not showing up for each other, not being emotionally available.

As I sat on the floor in front of him that day, I could see his emotion in his eyes, his throat closing as he simply nodded that we had to work on our relationship, that who we were was different and who we really are is different. In the instant I showed up, he met me there.

It was as if years of pain and disconnection evaporated between us in an instant. There was two people who loved each other, deeply, but were caught in worlds of conditioning, beliefs, trauma (trust me, he had plenty of his own stuff going on too!), life experiences, our fears, our shame, our guilt—who we are and how we show up and don't show up for each other.

The storm was over. As suddenly as it had come on, it was finished. I didn't know if I could trust it fully. I was always waiting for the next spiral. The next day, the next minute. The storm had been raging for so long I wasn't sure what this space was supposed to feel like. I wasn't ever in a space like this before. Not even "before" the phone call or the protein shake or the breakdown. I think my life was one series of breakdowns, and denial. This was new. And it was scarier than the storm.

I realized that enough stuff had come out of me, enough processing, emotional releasing had been done that I wouldn't go that low again. I was in a place where I could think again, where I could gain perspective.

The stress, the pain—it all lessened and I could think more clearly. And I knew I had to devise a plan. Now that I had allowed myself to see what was stored inside of me I needed to find a way to reconcile it all.

I created a plan to not only allow me to process the emotions but do something with them—turn them around—find the blessings and learn the lessons and let the rest go. I didn't want to keep living this life where I checked out, worked all the time and didn't live my life because I was too busy proving myself to get love and attention and respect.

I was ready for more. I was finally ready to live my life. I was ready to take charge of my life and stop living a fragmented life, like a bottle in the ocean banging off boats and rocks and being washed ashore and swept out again.

I was ready to design my life. I was ready to take charge, to create the life I wanted to live, to step into something new and not be a victim of circumstances or a game piece in someone else's life.

I was ready to stop seeing life through the filter of my own pain, my own perception because I had shut down, decided that people didn't care and that no one loved me, at a young age through the filter of trauma.

I was ready to see others for where they were and what they were also experiencing. I was ready to see that everyone is doing their best and most of us are just unprepared for the stuff that life brings to our doorsteps.

I was ready for life and allowing myself to let all of this stuff up that weighed me down and caused me to react the way I had been—by checking out and storing the experience in my body but never dealing with it, had opened me up to being able to live.

I sat quietly and asked for the guidance from the universe—help me understand this because I don't want to tow this stuff around forever and I don't want to be constantly in a state of releasing.

There's a time for releasing and there's a time for moving on.

Chapter Fifteen

ACCEPTANCE

I was ready to move on; to create something new. I was ready to turn my pain around into something more productive. I was ready to live from knowing not proving.

I began to write. I had been journaling and blogging but not like this. I hadn't written like this in decades. I had a poem to be published in a poetry book when I was 12. I was very excited. When I showed it to my mother and a relative, she responded, "*This sounds like a girl who was abused or something.*" I had been denying the abuse.

I destroyed the poem and didn't submit it. I didn't want it to be like that. I didn't want people to be able to know things, to see my shame. I didn't write like that again. I got acceptance and congratulations letters to university for English and even more while I was there, but I wasn't writing from my soul.

But a trip to the career counseling ended my English degree when I was told I could be a researcher or a teacher. I didn't want to be either. I was told there was no hope and no money in it as a career.

So, I changed majors and eventually got a *real* job, giving up writing. While I had been writing some and journaling as part of my healing, I wasn't sure my writing was good.

People always told me it was but it wasn't something I worked at and so I felt if I didn't have to work hard at it wasn't valid. But the message was writing. Write how I really felt, let it all out. And then find the truth in what was released.

When we hold onto things they turn toxic, they touch other things that are also not processed but similar and we build on them—"*see... I knew...* " Half of what we release is tangled up in our perception of it, our hurt and decades of other stuff with it.

When we release it all, we're releasing stuff that happened and then what we made it mean. Only when it's released can we begin to understand what it really means, what's the real truth to it. In *Rising strong* Brene Brown calls it the "s*** first draft" (SFD) and I adopted this principle to apply here.

Get it out. Who cares what it sounds like? Who cares what you say. Who cares how nasty or ugly or vile it is. It's better out than in. Plus, we don't keep the SFD. We burn it because we don't want anyone finding it, it's a self-preservation exercise, really. But it's also about releasing it, our willingness to tear out the pages and burn them is a willingness to let it go, let go of what we made it mean about us and a willingness to forgive those involved too. It's also ugly when it comes out and it's filled with anger, guilt, rage and often a lot of stuff that's not even the truth.

The next stage was to look for the truth. What is the real truth in that situation? There's the SFD, then there's the truth underneath it. For example, I'd often write in a frenzy until exhausted about what he or she or they did to me, how could they, how it made me feel. But the truth under that was I was angry at myself for not standing up for myself, for not defending myself.

Then came acceptance. Could I accept this? That this was the truth, that it really had nothing to do with someone else but I chose to allow in my life, that I chose to allow someone to treat me that way. Or sometimes I had to accept that the truth was the truth. It was a hard concept to swallow at times. I wanted it to be what they did to me. I wanted it to be what happened. Sometimes I wanted to hold onto it.

I liked the way it felt. I liked the way it hurt at times because it reminded me not to trust anyone, not to let my guard down, not to expect anything from anyone.

Holding onto resentment and the story that I made it mean meant I didn't have to feel the pain of what had actually happened. I was able to look away from that and hanging onto the anger was like holding onto the blade of the knife.

But the truth always wins. And eventually after kicking and screaming a bit over it and releasing it like an exorcism was happening, I could see that it wasn't really about what happened but about what I made it mean and how I held onto it and how I never said anything to stop it.

The truth can be hard to swallow but the saying "the truth shall set you free" exists for a reason. It really does give you freedom when you allow yourself to see it for what it really is.

The fourth step was to write a new story. What was I going to focus on, what lesson could I take from this? When I would find myself inevitably drawn back into victim mode and the blame game, what would I remind myself of until I had re-patterned the story.

You can't expect to learn something once and it's all better. Could I really be expected to just have it all better because I landed on it? Sometimes just uncovering the truth was enough to reframe and change it. But it was more common that it would return the next time something hit a trigger and if I didn't have something in place to help me through it and reframe it, I would be dragged into the old story.

Sometimes I had to go back into the old story dozens of times. I would later realize that it was because there was still stuff that had to be processed.

Chapter Sixteen

ACTION

We can only process things at the level we are. Which means sometimes we can't see the full picture of how a situation, a story or an experience impacted our lives all in one fell sweep. We might not realize how deep it runs until we learn more and revisit it.

Many things I processed and dealt with years ago have come back several times to be revisited and I'm sure they will return again as I continue to learn and grow into who I really am.

But without a plan, without writing a new story, it's easy to get caught up in the old one, to be brought down into the messiness of it. So, I always wrote a new story when I finished an SFD. The new story might be complex or short—a remembering of who I am, of what I wanted and needed to take from the experience.

And the fifth step was divine action. Inspired action. I always wanted the action to be something I didn't have to do with another person. I wanted it to be for me. Did I need to change my thoughts, change my perception? Sometimes action wasn't required. And sometimes it required a conversation with someone.

And that was the part I struggled with most. I'd write the action plan but would often leave it. I would just reframe it. But I came to learn nothing changes if nothing changes. I could reframe all day long but in the moments of being treated in ways that didn't feel good, steam rolled, walked on, intimidated if I didn't do something to change the conversation then nothing would change because I would be cycling through the s*** first draft, the truth, acceptance and a new story continuously.

Which I did for a time. And if I'm honest, I still get caught on that final one. Old habits really do die-hard and sometimes I still choose easy, sometimes I don't realize the lengths I will go to avoid speaking up, rocking the boat or making people uncomfortable.

But I do know unequivocally if we don't actively change anything, if we don't speak up, if we don't hard stop patterns and behaviors through divine and inspired action, then ultimately nothing will change and we will stay in the cycle.

I did realize I wasn't taking as much action as I was on the other 4 steps but I was healing and I allowed myself to be there. I was moving out of rock bottom and feeling better for the first time in a long time. I was doing things that made me happy, spending time with friends, writing, back exercising, I had switched to a plant-based diet without fear of what someone else might think. I was laughing again and taking on experiences that thrilled me, that pushed me out of my comfort zone like ziplining, walking on fire, travelling and mostly I was making friends, with old friends and new ones and I was falling in love with my husband all over again, this time as the real me.

I was making changes in how I showed up, how I spoke to people, how I viewed the world, my daily routine, what I accepted and didn't accept and I was transitioning away from the fitness industry into the world of the wild woman. I wasn't looking for permission or approval. I was finding myself, exploring the world as if with new eyes.

The dark night of the soul was over. I felt it. This was a good move forward and even if I wasn't fully doing all of the steps this place felt a lot better than anywhere I had ever been.

I wasn't living into or giving into everyone else's demands. I had an outlet for the things that were happening, my pen. It kept it from being stored and I could understand it. I could find the truth and take the good from it and let go of the bad. Even if I wasn't taking action all the time, this was a far better place than I had been.

For the first time in years I was truly feeling like a different person. I felt lighter, less dramatic, less hurt, less broken and less damaged. I had been so terrified of reliving these experiences thinking they would break me and that I wouldn't be able function but in reality, they helped me function.

Reliving these experiences and taking the perspective of what actually happened, what I made it mean about me and what I made it mean about others and what they thought about me and then how I pushed them away, gave me back my life.

I wasn't seeing it through the filter of a hurt child, I could see now that I had been processing everything as though I was that hurt child. I had a stunted growth, literally and figuratively. I'm a very short person but it became clear, emotionally I never grew.

To stop me from being hurt I fragmented, disassociated and become someone else. I decided that no one loved me, that no one cared and I created a fantasy world where people did.

When things happened in my life, I let them be with that side of me I never looked at. I shoved them into that place where I could pretend they didn't exist and then I could play in fantasy in another part of my brain. Never looking at, never seeing that I was living my life through the eyes of a hurt child.

Now that I had released so much of those experiences and was able to reframe them, understand that I had been operating on the emotional level of a child who had her arms crossed and stomping her feet, I felt free.

While I was still trying to understand this new world that had helped me through this in a way no therapy had been able to, I was also seeking out experiences that felt good to my soul. I was quitting things that didn't feel good and I was feeling less strange and more excited about this new world of healing that opened to me.

I felt the heartbeat of the earth, the connection to everything— the trees, the stars, the plants, and animals. I stopped hiding, stopped pretending and started looking inside for the answers.

The wild woman allows things to be what they are without needing to change them into something they are not. She looks at what she sees, she experiences the pain, she doesn't feel the need to make it into something it is not. She stands in the pain of it, learning and leaning in to find the lessons, the silver lining and she lets the pain transcend, helping her grow through it so it can teach her something about her.

Nothing else had given me this feeling. Combined with energy work and combinations of the work I had been studying for the last 3 years I finally felt like I was able to move forward.

I was rising.

And I was ready.

Chapter Seventeen

RISE

The fall is hard. It tears out of us everything we have been burying. The people in our lives don't always understand, we're changing, shedding the old and it's messy. Hell, we don't understand. Rock bottom is hard. It's hard to explain. It's hard to relate to others. It's hard to be there. And I'm sure hard to be around those who are at rock bottom.

I know before I experienced it myself I couldn't sit in someone else's pain. I know for those who have not allowed themselves the process of breaking down, or for those who never changed themselves to fit in, cannot possibly understand what it's like to be there.

I looked for support. I looked for help in places I thought it should be. It wasn't there. I was told I was addicted to the breakdown or that I was "still" there. My fall started in late 2014 and by late 2015 I was rising. 1 year through the worst of it—to deal with and process my abuse and other problems that I had never dealt with.

I wanted approval, I wanted support, I wanted understanding. I wanted someone to care. I went to those who I thought should care. But I wanted something from someone who couldn't understand, and when I went to someone who *could* understand, who didn't judge me but simply let me be in the mess of it, that's when I finally began to heal.

I was not shamed or made feel like I should be somewhere else. I had spent 34 years pretending everything was fine, pretending I was someone I was not. I was allowed to be here, feeling this. It was not the time to put my big girl pants on. It was time to stop getting up, stop being ok, stop pretending to be *fine*, all the time.

But when we allow ourselves to truly fall, not pretend fall, not sort of fall, but the type of fall that makes you wonder if you'll ever get up, the fall that breaks your knee caps, the kind that has you gasping for air and sobbing at the same time…the fall that breaks you wide open so your soul can cry….

Only then can we rise. In that fall we will be stripped of everything that we pretended. Once we are stripped bare, exposed, raw and empty we can then design life. We are no longer those children who were conditioned to behave and listen and be good and not speak up or out line. Now we can choose what life we want to create.

As I began to feel better I embarked on another soul experience— Date with Destiny with Tony Robbins, a personal and professional development expert. This would be my 3rd Tony experience. I had taken all of his online and DVD programs and this was now my 3rd live event. I wasn't sure what to expect, each other one broke me open in ways I wasn't expecting and DWD, as it's lovingly referred, was supposed to be the best one.

Was I ready? Could I do this? I had started feeling better. What if I was more broken by this, like when I had been to his Vegas program? What if it made things worse? What I fell, again?

I did.

It's a stir you up and put you back together program. My work with my shaman, my writing, and the processes I had been working on and working through had prepared me for this. I felt as though I understood on a profound level everything that was happening.

I'm not sure that I would have gotten as much from DWD if I hadn't worked with my healer. Many of Tony's teachings in DWD were very spiritual and shamanic and healing based without him saying so.

I was reacting strongly to things—a lot of stuff I thought I had released—more layers came up. I had to take deeper looks at my beliefs about myself, the things that happened to me, who I had become, what I believed, what I wanted, and if I was really ready to let go and move into the life that I knew I was here to live.

As the program went on I began to experience physical symptoms. My stomach bloated and swelled. My clothes wouldn't fit and I was in physical pain. I had a headache that wouldn't release and I began to get sores inside my mouth. My gums were blistering and my tongue had gotten sores all over it.

I couldn't explain it. I was a mess. I was overwhelmed, exhausted from no sleep, no food and all of the emotional things that was being stirred up.

We store the emotions physically and when we release things and bring it up, it also releases it from our physical body.

I felt as if I were afraid to miss something, the energy was static, palpable. I could feel it. I was afraid I wouldn't learn something and the whole week would be a waste and I would never get better, I would be stuck in this vortex forever. That morning my shaman sent me a message that my jaguar spirit animal was travelling with me and I could call on him anytime I needed. I was feeling particularly raw that day.

Driving to the conference center I wanted to punch my roommate in the face, everything was annoying me. I was so frustrated and irritated. Not because of anything she was doing but because I was feeling so off, stirred up and annoyed. I've never been a violent person but I felt sick to my stomach, we were late and I was going to miss my team meeting and I was feeling bloated, extreme fatigue and annoyed. I put my headset on and took deep breaths as I just focused on calming myself.

At the lights I felt my eyes drawn to a building and as I looked up there was the Jaguar car dealership with a giant jaguar logo staring at me. I felt uneasy, like something was about to happen. As we pulled into the conference center a bus passed by with the cougar logo on it.

A car passed in front of me with plates 777 on it. 777 has different meaning for everyone, commonly seen as abundance and good luck, but for me, 777 was just another repeating number, these are signs I see a lot of. Repeating number series for me are like finding dimes for others— protected, connected.

I felt like I was in a movie and everything was in slow motion. There were signs everywhere. I felt surreal, scared and uncertain but my mood did not improve and I was not using any of the tools I had been learning to help me feel better.

I met with my team lead and had a full-blown meltdown. I couldn't think, I was scared, I was resisting some of the deeper work we were asked to do. So, we had a session, where my team leader explained some more things to me and I started seeing how I was only focusing on the negative because I was scared to open up, really open up to anyone else, to life itself. The story of being broken kept me in the fear. I was seeing me as broken and therefore anything in my life as broken, my business, relationship, friendships, all broken. What if I could create the life I really wanted if I was willing to step into the unknown? What were the good things about him, about us, about business, my life, my pain, even.

Things began shifting. I realized that I took things and made it everything. It played everything into my belief that people will hurt you; people don't care. I forgot all the great things. This wasn't rose colored glasses off. It was negative glasses on. What else was this about?

As the day progressed, I continued to feel worse. I was panicking. I could feel the energy of something about to happen and I couldn't relax into the experience Tony was taking us through. As my energy and panic rose I remembered the Jaguar.

Despite months of work with my shaman, I still wasn't sure how I felt about it all. I wasn't even sure if I believed it, but I practiced it because it was helping. This was the first time I called on the power animal outside of a session with my shaman.

I asked him to help me relax and just forget about what else was happening. One thing wasn't going to ruin this week and I asked Jaguar to help me just chill out because my anxiety, overwhelm and stress were on bust.

And instantly I was transported, again. I was no longer in the room with 3000 people. I was in a house, a hallway. I was frantically opening and closing doors but they were all locked. I didn't recognize it but I knew it in my soul, as though I had been there before.

My jaguar was with me as I walked the hallway. I had seen this in another meditation. I had seen this very hallway and me searching this hallway but I had not found an unlocked door.

This time at the very end was an unlocked door. I was scared to open the door but my jaguar nudged me along. I could feel its energy, it's power, and its presence reminding me I was safe. As I stepped into the room I didn't see anything, it was empty. It felt anti climatic. I could feel the anticipation leading up to it. Half the room was shrouded in light and half in darkness.

It reminded me of a castle turret. But there was nothing to see. I didn't understand but turned to leave, feeling confused, why was the door open this time if there was nothing in there? And I turned to go, something caught my attention in the darkness. I was scared to go but I was reminded Jaguar has the ability to see in the dark and was my protector. I was safe.

As I stepped into the darkness my eyes adjusted and I knew I had been here before. Then I saw it, the birdcage and inside, me. I was wasting away. A bedraggled waif of a girl about 10 years old, scared, alone and hoarse from being suffocated and silenced, and malnourished from being starved, not starved physically, but soul starved.

It was the real me. I had locked up her up and thrown away the key. Being made fun of, not accepted, bullied, abused, and being too naïve and soft had turned me into someone I wasn't. I couldn't survive that and I had lost the fun part, the naïve part, the happy, playful, loving part. I had become hardened.

I changed who I was to be liked, to be normal, to be accepted.

I did it to protect myself. I could see that now. The hope on her face, the excitement, it sickened me. That was the part of me that I hid for a reason—the fool who was so gullible, who was so easily manipulated and used. Here she was, locked up for more than 2 decades and still happy to see me.

This was where I had left her, me, when I became someone else— the don't give a f*** girl was formed here, when I donned a new shell and I became a shell of a person.

Was I hoping someone would save me? Was I hoping someone would notice? Or was I truly tired of being made fun of? I wanted to be the girl who couldn't be hurt. So, I became her. I decided to be someone else and I emerged differently at that age, the darkened butterfly.

As I stared at her, I both pitied and resented her. I was scared I would become that pitiful made fun of awkward girl I used to be. The funny thing is I always thought becoming harder, not caring was going to lead me to the life I really wanted. But in reality, it led me to everything I didn't want.

When you pretend not to care, people treat you like you don't care and you can't say anything because you've got an image to protect. Becoming the girl who didn't care meant I was surrounded by people who accepted that I didn't care. They thought I didn't care. I have learned that people believe what you show them.

I'm sure people over the years saw through me. But I've also learned that most people are too busy, caught up in their own stuff to notice. If they do notice and you say you're *fine* they accept it at face value. We all do it, maybe we don't want to get into it, maybe we think they don't want our help, maybe they think all kinds of things, who knows? What I know is that when you pretend not to care, people think you don't care and treat you like you don't care.

No one is coming to save you. No one is going to break down the walls that you build except you. No one is going to fight enough for you because no matter what they when you're in that place will not be enough. They could climb the turret walls and you'd smash their fingers and ask them to climb up bloodied and beaten and still say they didn't care or didn't work hard enough or come fast enough.

There isn't enough caring or fighting for you when you cannot see it, when you are bent on seeing the worst and believing that no one cares. I believed no one cared. I believed no one would come for me. And when people got close to me I smashed the windows on their fingers and pushed them away. I wanted to be left alone.

I was standing in the moment it started. I had been leaving my body for a long time by the time I was 10. I was checking out regularly, like many abuse victims do. I would turn off and create fantasies in my mind of a different life. I would play out movies in my mind, dream of being somewhere else so I could detach. I would play house in my mind.

It's why I have almost no memories of it. I wasn't there. While the abuse had stopped and my abuser was no longer around, I had never admitted it so I never got the freedom others got for telling. I began living an outright lie.

I stopped going to family events. I stopped going out to play and started spending all of my time in my room. I was dreaming of better things, a better life, one day when I could eventually leave here.

It was all I did. Read and dream of better days. I didn't interact with anyone that I didn't have to. I made it look good on the outside, I had friends, I went out, I was involved in groups and programs and I got A's. But I became obsessed with my eating disorder. I counted my ribs and I organized my closets by color. I made food the enemy.

As a teenager, I became obsessed with boys and my body. I wanted to be wanted. Wanted to be needed. And the one guarantee was through sex appeal. I wanted to be desired and the only way I knew how was through sex.

So, I threw her away. I threw me away; to fit in; to not care; to not be hurt. I wore amour. I expected nothing so got nothing in return. I acted like I didn't care so I was treated like I didn't care.

As suddenly as I had left, I was called back to the stadium, to my chair in the middle of the row. I don't know what journey the room took but I took a wild ride to the depths of where I had been hiding the real me. We were instructed to journal and write about our experience. So, I made my way to the aisle of the conference room.

As I wrote, the magnitude of it all hit me. And I sobbed from my soul. I had never cried like that before. I didn't think I would make it, as deep-wrenching sobs came from me. I needed someone but I couldn't even get up to find help, and asking for help wasn't my strong suit. So, I prayed. I still didn't know if I believed in God but I knew if there was a God and he could help me now was the time I needed a miracle.

As quickly as I had asked a set of arms embraced me. And I leaned in—for the first time in my life I leaned in and I let someone I didn't know hold me. As I cried for the little girl I was, the child I never got to be, the innocence robbed and lost not only by sexual abuse but by a cruel world full of cruel people who liked to hurt people or who at the very least were trying to get rid of me because of the dirtied reputation I had based on the abuse.

Everyone says *you did nothing wrong* but is that true when you're treated like there is very much something wrong with you? I imprisoned myself in an effort to fit in, to be enough I had created the version of me that existed today. The shell, the armor, the person I had become was all because I wanted to be someone else, someone who would fit in, not care, not be able to be reachable or hurt.

I had closed myself off from living because it was too painful. But the long-term result was suffering more by being someone else than I ever had in being myself.

I had developed sinus issues over the years and always sounded like I had a cold. As I sobbed I felt something release in my forehead and I released years' worth of stuff. I literally let myself snot and bawl into someone. I held on for dear life. The sessions were back underway and there we were, this woman and myself locked in an embrace for what felt like eternity.

Finally, I was done crying. I felt empty, exhausted, as though I cried tears that I had held in my whole life. (I have never had a sinus issue again unless I'm emotionally blocked. Anytime my sinuses act up, I know that I have something brewing that will need to be worked through.) As the seminar had already started, I made my way back to my chair, not getting her name or knowing who she was.

I realized so many things in that moment. Despite the fact that I was "doing" the shamanic healing world I was scared to share it with a lot of people. I was afraid of being judged. And I was even more scared of being called crazy. But here I was, having called on jaguar medicine on my own and invoked myself to take a spiritual journey in the middle of 3000 people, by myself. It was the first time I had relaxed and let go. Letting my guard down wasn't something I did well.

I still didn't know what to think about any of this stuff, but like the clearing work I had been doing—I was feeling stronger and better, so I went with it.

I had a new perspective on God, the universe and what was happening. I later tracked down the woman who had shown up for me that day. She was a team leader on another team. I reached out to her to say thank you and ask her how she ended up there. She said she felt she had to walk down that aisle, someone needed her and while there were hundreds of people on the floor, she knew it was me; something told her.

How can I explain this experience other than for what it is? I was a non-believer for a long time, so many of the experiences I had left me uncomfortable with God. How could a God exist and have the things we have in our world—abuse, rape, crime, and murder? How could God watch those things happen and do nothing. But this one left me with a profound knowing that something beyond me had just orchestrated this whole thing. The entire day was surreal with symbolism. I knew I was being guided.

I stopped crying that day when I was finished crying. Not when it was convenient. I didn't care that I stood out or that the speaker had started again. I didn't follow the rules to fit in and be good. I just let myself cry it out right there on the floor. That was a huge shift for me, to let myself be and do what I needed to do.

When I returned to my seat I felt an excitement take over my body. I was worried I would miss something important and ended up on the most amazing journey I had ever experienced because I decided to let go and let myself experience what I had.

The sores in my mouth cleared up that night, my belly flattened out and my sinuses cleared up. I had diarrhea for hours after and into the next day, I couldn't leave the bathroom and a call to my spiritual teacher told me that it was my body literally releasing stuff I've held onto, how I had given up my power.

As it turns out the power center—the 3ʳᵈ chakra—where our power resides right at the stomach was releasing the emotional blocks. I had always had stomach issues which I blamed on the eating disorders but the eating disorders now made sense—feeling hungry, feeling the emptiness made me feel powerful and strong—it was a fake strength because my real strength was given up when I threw myself away.

To this day when I'm working through anything that has caused me to give up my power I experience an immense physical release. And I've seen it happen to many other people who begin to reclaim their power. As we release the experiences that caused us to give up our power, what we have been holding onto is also released and we can restore order to the chakras in a healthy way.

Chapter Nineteen

(UN)BECOME

I found myself. I knew exactly what had happened, that I had intentionally become someone else, someone I wasn't, I changed my personality, my beliefs, how I behaved, how I let people treat me, what I allowed and tolerated—all to be the person who couldn't and wouldn't be hurt. But in reality, I was just taking it all and putting into this black box and I had become a shell of a person.

I was dead while alive. I was living in gray when I desperately wanted color. I wanted love and romance and passion but I settled for surface dwelling, trading sex for love. I wanted friendship and connection but I acted like I didn't care. I wouldn't put myself out there because I was afraid people would see the broken bits and decide, like my childhood friends, that I was broken.

If I could hide it and I could find ways to be successful then I could prove that I was good enough somehow.

It all made sense now—the masks, the armor I wore became noticeable. I couldn't deny them anymore. I could feel them, the weight of them, how heavy it was. I was not who I pretended to be. I could feel the disconnection. I was now acutely aware of the problem.

Rock bottom was over. I knew it. I now had faith that things were going to get better. I knew things were going to improve because now I profoundly understood that I had to become me…now was my chance to decide who I got to be, to cut the cords, to release the triggers and choose a new outcome, a new future by my willingness to show up for myself.

Like a caterpillar who had crawled into the cocoon, thinking they were about to die, but just in the moment they believed it was all over, they were reborn.

How would I rise, really rise? Who did I need to become in order to live the life I was here to live? How could I know myself after all of these years? I was a child when I changed who I was. I felt like I could be the changeling. I changed, my soul was stolen, blocked, and now that I could see that I knew profoundly my work was to become her, not just know about her and visit her or leave her there, but it was now time to breathe life into her, to give her life, to let her grow and be nourished.

To become the same person, not a divided person who decided who to be based on who I was with or the situation. Now it was time to find out who I was and become the same person no matter where I was or who I was with, no more changing to be pleasing or fitting in.

What did I like? What did I want? Who was I? I felt an immense duality in this situation as I felt disconnected and yet more connected. I had begun the journey home, but wasn't quite aware of that.

Now was my time to create the life I wanted to live instead of playing pretend and just being swept up in, a pawn in other people's stories, a footnote. I wasn't born to be a footnote. It was time to be the leading lady in my life not just accepting bit pieces anymore.

As I began to speak up, express myself and speak my truth it didn't always go as I hoped. I suppose I didn't account for the fact that I had been this way for so long that everyone in my life was just used to things being as they had been.

Other people didn't have the experiences I had and so my words, my behavior, my changing wasn't welcome and not understood. I lost people. I was told I was being negative. I was told to dull it down.

They didn't know that I was unbecoming all that I was not. They said I was different and I was, I was changing, growing, finding my own footing, saying no to things I had always yes to and yes to things I had always been so scared of.

While the destruction that followed might have seemed like my rock bottom to some, it was actually my rising. Finding ourselves is one thing but being it is quite another. Even when we find ourselves, when we go into that cave and explore the places we had turned off, hidden and how we dulled ourselves to fit, now choosing the new way, letting die what must die, and welcoming back the parts of us that had buried, isn't easy.

I began to say no, to say how I felt, to go after what I wanted, and asked to be treated differently. Allowing myself to voice my feelings, to work through and release emotionally, to move toward what I really wanted to do, to have the courage to step out of the box and create the life I really wanted—go after my dreams, the real dreams not the watered-down version that seems safer or more approved or that I didn't have to fight for.

I prepared, I planned, I wrote, I healed, I helped, I moved, I took off band aids, I cut out parts that didn't belong, I cried, I kicked, I screamed, I prayed, I meditated, I journeyed, I visualized and I felt the falling away of all that wasn't me. I felt the armor dropping off piece by piece.

That me was how I survived what I didn't think I could survive, she helped me close my heart and become the tin woman. My biggest challenge was letting her go. I didn't want to let her go, she was my security blanket, she was me, the only me I knew. I was still struggling with my identity—if I wasn't this, what was I?

What if I got hurt, what if I was too naïve and stupid and couldn't do this on me own? What if my heart led me astray? This armor was my shrewdness.

The struggle was real. I could feel the battle for keeps, the part of me that wanted to sink into it, walk away, put the walls back up and just coast. I didn't want to be vulnerable, real or give anyone the capacity to hurt me. I didn't want to be weird. I wanted to punish people who hurt me, by withdrawing from them, from life, pushing them away.

But I had tasted that freedom of being me. The freedom that comes when you know your soul, when you have felt yourself after decades, when you have let go of the masks, the cloaks, the outfits and you have looked into your very soul and know who you are and why you exist.

I couldn't go back to that empty, lonely existence of safety. I was safe but I wasn't living; I was numb, dead inside. I wanted to breathe, to have fun, to be free and be my wild untamed self.

The process of unbecoming who I was to be who I am was a process of destruction, burning it all down, tearing it all apart, cha cha'ing—some days being the warrior and other days being the frightened little girl who didn't know what to do so I did nothing, I froze, like trauma victims do.

Some days I ran, I overreacted, I under reacted and some days I just did nothing except exist. I was recreating myself. Tearing apart who we became, to cope, isn't an easy process. It's not a pretty meditating love and light process. It's a battle of dark and light. And while there is a romanticizing of this process—of finding yourself—I can promise you, the new you will cost you the old you. And that process of dying and being born again is painful.

The storm is violent, it's heartbreaking, it's overwhelming. And many people stop the process. They don't continue because they think there is something wrong with them. They medicate, they avoid, and they eat. But the only way through the storm is to keep going.

In my life I never walked around talking about my experiences that had impacted and influenced me. I talked about meaningless stuff, I talk about people, I griped about the world and what was wrong with the people in it. I complained about work and money and all of those things that everyone talks about.

My cousin once told me that she had no idea how she was living before doing self-development work. She said, *"I have no idea how I was living, making decisions or getting through life"*. I understood exactly what she meant. I wasn't making decisions. I wasn't engaged. I was in constant reaction to my life and the things that were happening but I never actively designed my life. I never asserted myself. I was reactive. I was passive aggressive, but I was never assertive. I let other people choose. I let other people decide. I went along with.

I did what I thought I was supposed to do all the time. I looked to others for guidance, approval, validation. And I often didn't get it, not in the way I wanted it or needed.

In life, I took everything so personally. With friends, work, jobs, relationships. I held onto everything that happened, stored it inside and everything that happened in life hit all of those unprocessed things.

I felt an immense amount of stress to earn a certain amount of money so I could justify living my dream. I listened to everyone else tell me who to be to do that. The customer is always right so every complaint I was going way over board to fix it. I had people who figured out if they complained about something they would get a discount. They complained every month, not because there was something wrong, but because they could manipulate me, because I would never say anything to them.

I saw so much ugliness in people. I didn't realize it was all an opportunity for me to say I won't trade my peace or myself or my worth for this. I was operating from fear. I was keeping poisonous and toxic people in my life and letting them plant seeds of fear that I needed to put up with bad behavior in order "to make it".

I had people spreading lies and rumors about me. And even worse in my classes while I was there, making comments like "*who does she think she is charging that kind of money?*" And even though I was told these things, I never did anything to defend myself. I had people tell me to my face that they heard I wasn't a good trainer. They didn't mind telling me the things that would hurt me. And the problem is I believed them and I fought to be better, to be good enough, to prove myself, instead of asking them to leave or standing up for myself.

Which only made things worse. My confidence was eroded. My happiness, my goodness, was all eroded. The problem was not what they said, it was that I believed it.

Instead of turning those people out of my life, I set a place at the table for them. Come in, pull up a chair, and abuse me. It feels like home. It's a place I know well. What do you want from me? Let me get that for you. And when I'd turn around, stabbed in the back. I'd simply hand back the knife and apologize for making them stab me, and let them do it over and over again.

Because I believed there was always something wrong with me. Opening the business was both a blessing and a curse because it was what led to my ultimate breakdown and eventually my breakthroughs and to where I am today.

It helped me down but I had to face all of that in order to create and live the life I wanted really. And it helped me up. I love the woman I am today. I have walked through the dark night, through the eye of the storm to become her.

Chapter Twenty

PURGE

The process of rising was harder than I imagined because in the rise we're trying new things, and in the trying of the new things, we're coming up against more of those things that are still there. The clean-up process, like a residue being scraped from the bottom of a barrel.

Do I like this? Do I want this? Who am I really? What are my values, beliefs? What do I believe in? What beliefs needs to go? What beliefs need to be installed?

If I were to allow myself to dream, what would I dream? If I stopped looking for permission and approval and validation, what would happen? What experiences and beliefs need to be rewritten now that I could use my mind again? Now that the purging of the emotions was gone and I was ready to emotionally grow past 10.

I just didn't have it in me anymore to care about the pettiness of it all. I cared about my soul, my health, my happiness, my vibration. I wanted to know about my soul and other people's soul. I wanted to feel connected. I wanted to feel alive. I wanted to feel like I was actually living instead of talking about living or waiting to live until....

I adopted a lot of wild women traits. The ability to see things for what they are, no need to change them. I stopped conforming and said no. A lot. I also said yes, a lot. I stepped into the wild woman, I embraced her. I let the chips fall where they may. I stirred the pot, rocked the boat and burned the bridges.

I pulled out old memories that left imprints on my soul, things I remembered now that I hadn't been able to before, things that held me back in ways I didn't even realize until they were out.

When I was a little over 2 my second youngest brother was born. He was a preemie. And my mother was gone a lot. I was just a baby and I remember watching her walk down the driveway and I was scared. I had never been without her I suppose and now I didn't know when she was coming back.

She was in the hospital and my brother was in there a long time. When he finally came home I remember him in a basinet on the floor model stereo we had. I reached up and grabbed the basinet and turned it, and him, into the floor. He cried, everyone started screaming and I hid under my bed.

Until recently I had only remembered that I was bad. A relative there said I was jealous and wanted to hurt him and I remember hiding under the bed. I was so scared.

Those' words played over and over in my mind. I always remembered my fingers on his cradle and those words. A moment of impact, as I like to call them. These moments that stand out to us when something happened. We might not remember everything but there's an image, a memory, frozen into us.

During a memory recovery session to help me find some of my earliest, most painful memories, when I had made decisions about myself and the world around me, I landed on that memory.

It's the first memory I have. Me hurting my baby brother who had just gotten out hospital after being born premature with bronchitis and a host of other medical problems.

I wasn't up for a sister of the year award.

But as I sank into the memory I looked for the positive intent. What was happening right before that? Why did I go the bassinet, what was I really after? And I remembered that I had just wanted to see him. He was perfect. I loved him instantly and I wanted to look at him again.

I didn't know I could hurt him. I didn't understand the consequences of my actions. But the words used to describe me during the event, bad and jealous became the storyline of my life.

I was a bad person.

So, when I was being abused I thought it was my punishment. I thought I had done something wrong and this was my punishment. When I was being questioned, I thought it was my fault. My grandmother had said not to go there and I did.

I deserved it. It wasn't his fault; it was mine. I shouldn't have gone there. Frozen in time, book bag in hand, staring up, trying not to get in trouble if they found out it was my fault.

Uncovering these memories changed my life. It gave me access to the real intent; the real feelings behind things. I realized I wasn't driven by anger or resentment or jealously. I was driven by love. I wanted to see him and hold him. I wanted to love him.

The conclusions we draw can be spelled out for us by others or they can be decided by us. We might decide what something means and accept it as our truth. For me, as a two-year-old that wasn't possible. But I could go back and reclaim the memory, my truth, from that experience and release the false one that I had believed because someone else didn't know my intent.

As long as I believed I was not good enough, I would always be trying to prove myself. Now, I can look back and connect all the dots of what led to my breakdown, what I was storing and how I was spending my life spinning my wheels trying to prove myself to be good enough.

I was recreating systems, cycles and patterns over and over again so I could learn the lessons, so I could wake up and heal the wounded parts of me so I could see that because some bad things happened that I wasn't bad. And that not everything everyone else believed or saw had to be my truth.

I can see now why things didn't work.

PART 4
FINDING A VOICE

I wasn't born to be a footnote
—Tonya Whittle

Chapter Twenty-One

SHIFT

The darkness isn't a bad place. What we've forgotten is in there. Who we are is in there; it's buried under the experiences and the beliefs we formed about the world and ourselves. If we can let it teach us we can learn from it and change our lives.

Life is hard. It's going to throw us things we can't begin to imagine. It's going to break us down with the life experiences and lessons. I always asked *"why me? Why does everything have to go wrong?"* And one day as I was journaling I had the answer—*"Why not me? Why should someone else have this story and not me? Who would you suggest for the job, Tonya"* flew out of my pen.

Maybe I was born to help change and shift this paradigm of hiding who we are and believing the negative, the bad things about ourselves. I wrote: *"when are you going to start seeing the good, when are you going to start seeing the humanity, when are you going to stop proving yourself and accept that you are already enough? When are you going to realize that if someone else thinks that what happened to you broke you, that it's their problem not yours. When are you going to see the beauty in the darkness, the beauty in the pain that you have endured? When are you going to see these scars as evidence of what you've survived and were able to get through and how resilient, strong and amazing you are? When are you going to start expecting good things to happen? When are you going to believe in yourself?"*

I was waiting for someone else to tell me I was enough, that I could do this, that I was capable. I was waiting for approval and permission.

It was time to stop waiting for someone else to say I was enough. It was time to shift my beliefs, how I saw myself and how I saw what happened to me.

1 in 4.

My story isn't mine alone. My story is the same as so many other people's stories. I didn't want that story so I rejected it. And in rejecting what happened to me I rejected who I was. I rejected a part of myself because I believed that part was shameful, something wrong with it. And if I could hide it and become successful in spite of it, it wouldn't matter.

But it did matter and it does matter. It's a part of me. It made me who and what I am today. It shaped my early childhood experiences. It robbed me of my innocence. And it robbed me of a life of believing in myself, of knowing my worth, knowing my value.

Who I became and the choices I made were a result of that. It wasn't just something bad that happened that didn't matter. In denying the truth I was rejecting myself. I was telling myself that I was not good enough, that I was broken, damaged for it. And I was terrified of being pitied, of having myself and my family judged. I felt like I would wear the scarlet letter.

If people knew this would I just become the girl who had been abused? Would I ever be more than that?

But now I know, I was more than that. It wasn't about what happened to me but it was about living anyway. It was about choosing to still go after what I wanted. It was about thriving and not merely surviving. It was about owning all of myself and the things that make up who I am.

The truth heals. What we hide hurts us because it causes us to reject ourselves, our very existence, we lose parts of ourselves, parts of our soul in the rejection of ourselves. It turns toxic; our body stores the pain of that and our physical symptoms are often signing of an emotional and spiritual root. We are constantly looking for something to fill that void—food, people, anything to complete us.

But nothing outside of us can complete us until we bring back all parts of ourselves—especially the parts that we rejected as something foul. When we call those parts back, we feel whole.

I had to believe that I was good enough. I had to believe in me. I had to write a new story that was born from exploring the darkness. I had to write a new story in which all the parts of me were here—no more duality. Just me, as I am.

I let the darkness teach me. While I had released so much stuff I didn't think there was anything left to that black hole, there was. As I started to write that new story, choosing a new path, the old stuff, the triggers and fears and experiences that had caused me to shut down came for me.

Each time I went to a new level, I had to work through them. If you are working through trauma, every new level will require a new version of you. You will be required to grow into the person you want to be. If you set a goal to do something that you have never done you need to become the version of you who can achieve it.

That may mean fighting some old demons that have told you that you can't, that it's better to not try, or give up and not care. But you'll be strong enough. Like I was. I was ready for this. And while it was hard I faced the journey head on, not all days were great but I was moving steadily in the direction of my dreams. My light had to shine brighter than my biggest fear.

You will break down the walls; the barriers, the beliefs and you will see it all for what it is. And then, you will write a new story. Then you will stand in that new story, letting the old fall away and the new come in.

The in between is not comfortable—unsure of who you are but knowing who you are not. There is the space that few talk about between the not anymore and not yet, the messy middle ground. The breakdown is heard and the finish is beautiful but the middle is messy as you unbecome and become. It's not comfortable, but comfortable is not what we're here to do, wild one.

In order to rise we have to work through that stuff, we have to clear it away, clear our energy, clear the trauma's, clear life's conditioning to remove the masks and the armor we wear. We cannot rise while we're still carrying all of that old baggage.

Becoming who we are is the privilege of a lifetime.

So, few get to do it. But the energy of a new paradigm is here. No longer are we the robots listening to what we're told, changing who we are to fit because somewhere along the way we learned to feel shame for the things that happened to us.

We're here to ushering in a new way of being where self-awareness, emotional intelligence, standing for who you are, and breaking the silence is the norm.

We are better than this world that we've created by living in silence and shame. Whether you have been silent and shamed or whether you've been the silencer and the shamer, it's time to stop. We are better than the destruction and the greed we have been succumbing to. We are better than the slaughter that happens at our hands and we are better than the corruption. We are better than forcing people to be silent and not letting people speak up.

We are better than forcing people to change and be something they're not. And we're better than changing to fit in where we don't belong.

This isn't about being a victim. This is about the truth. It's not about the first draft being the story we tell, it's about the truth we speak. When we own our story, we get to write the ending. When we refuse to own our story, we become victim to it. Allowing it to be healed gives us back our power.

We have been frightened for centuries, enslaved by the elitists who carried the power to torture and execute us. Science shows us that trauma changes our DNA, living in fear every day changes our response to trauma and changes our resilience. Becoming who we are not in order to survive changes us and changes our future generations through changed DNA. Advances in modern science has opened up a new world to us. Understanding and seeing the brain change in response to trauma, especially childhood trauma is huge for us moving forward to create a better world.

Our brain's response literally changes. Parts of the brain doesn't develop properly.

There are monsters among us and they exist because we allow them to. I remember hearing an extended family member say "*why didn't she keep her mouth shut*" when the abuse had been reported to the police.

As it turns out, I discovered 24 years later that it wasn't that family member at all that had reported it. It was someone different. But because she was the one always speaking up against stuff, she was blamed for it.

I don't even know if anyone actually asked who reported it or how it was found out. Silence and shame go hand in hand. Back then it was still common practice to hide everything that was shameful. Mind your own business; keep your nose out of it. It's these mentalities that allow predators among us. Why didn't she keep her mouth shut?

They were more concerned about what people thought than the children being abused. *Let that sink in for a minute.*

I'm so grateful someone finally did speak up and our family was thrown into chaos because of it. But a lot of people knew and only one did something.

This conversation is the very same one that allows people to drive drunk without being reported. It's the same one that allows child porn and animal abuse to continue. Because there is a belief that you should remain silent, that you shouldn't get involved, that it's none of your business, even when it *is* your business.

Because abuse of any kind is all of our business.

It's those people who choose to rise anyway, those who choose to stand up and speak up and risk their own fitting in, their own safety, their own inclusion because inclusion that comes at the cost of looking the other way isn't worth the scars it leaves on your soul.

I know family members knew. I know neighbors knew or suspected. Their children weren't allowed to play at our place. Discovering the same person had abused other family members was placed carefully in the black hole. I didn't want to disturb that one. That was a biggie and when it came back up to be dealt with there were a lot of s first drafts written about it.

As an adult I understand that they had also been abused. They were living in their own trauma. But the child inside of me couldn't understand how they could know and not do anything about it?

It's why I cannot look away from suffering or heart-breaking abuse. It's why I'll always stand up, even if I stand alone and even if everyone thinks I'm wrong and should sit back down.

Because I know what it feels like to realize people knew and chose not to do anything about it. I cannot look the other way. I cannot look away from suffering. Forgiveness is a beautiful thing because I do not hold grudges; I truly understand and empathize. And I hope none of my family, or anyone who did know, does not carry shame and guilt for it because it doesn't serve anyone. And they only operated from their own place, their own trauma, their own triggers, their own wounds as well as the conditions of times they lived in.

And I am grateful for those who decided to move forward, to not try to hide it. And I'm grateful and sorry for those who didn't know and who were the ones thrown into the clean-up of it, the holding it together, the ownership of it, wearing the scarlet letter. Because that was brave. That was courage. That was fear without an out. That was thrown into a storm no one can prepare you for.

We all become something—wear some form of armor to help us cope with the trauma we experienced. We don't always know why we make the choices we do, except that it's from a place of fear, survival, or down right denial. And when we realize we've been living there and what happened when we were, it can be a big blow. I know it well from my own place.

I carried a lot of shame and guilt for not speaking up when I had the chance. People today say I'm so courageous and there's still that voice that comes in *I wasn't courageous when I needed to be. I was a coward then.* As I embarked on the journey of writing this book I questioned if I had the right to tell this story because I had not told the truth back then.

It took a lot of work to realize that this is my story, as I lived it and that I have a right to tell it. Not only a right but also a duty because my life was vastly different because I rejected the truth of being abused.

Because I refused to own my story I became a victim to it, always protecting it, making sure I never let anything slip, leaving places where it might come up, keeping my distance from my family for fear it might come up.

I never let anyone else tell his or her stories. I was a silencer. It was a big surprise when I realized that having conversations about things we're not supposed to was part of my purpose.

I was the person who silenced other people, who suggested there is a "time and a place" because I didn't want people to know my stuff, I didn't want to be in the space and the discomfort of it.

Who I became as a result of not owning my story, not admitting the truth was a different story than those who admitted it, saw and felt justice. Justice happened for me too, but not because of my courage. I wasn't courageous back then. I wanted to save myself.

I rejected my family and myself. I pushed people away. I became someone who I didn't recognize and I'm sure they didn't either. I distanced myself and detached and disassociated from everything. As I began to rise into myself, to rebuild my life I had to be who I was. I had to be open to learning and growing and saying what I liked and didn't like. That was weird and new for everyone because I had been ok with things for 30 years that now I was saying was not ok.

My grandfather told me before he passed on that he had always been worried about me. He said he noticed a big change in me, how I went from being full of laughter and smiles and sunshine and just a happy child, to a dark brooding, angry, pushing everyone away person.

He told me he wanted to do something but he didn't know what to do. That he didn't know how to reach me. And I cried that day because I knew it was true; that I had chosen to separate from my family. I wanted to put distance between them and me and the shame I felt.

I wanted to hold onto looking normal and feeling normal. I wanted to not be hurt. And in rejecting the parts of me, I also rejected my family. I didn't listen to the stories anymore. I became a crusty, cranky, high strung girl with eating disorders and anger issues.

I told myself repeatedly that no one cared. That they didn't love me. That it didn't matter if I lived or died. And eventually when you push people away for so long, they go. They leave.

No one can help someone who doesn't want to be helped. I wanted to be angry. I wanted to be left alone. I wanted to push them away and punish them. I wanted them to feel as bad as I did. I wanted someone to save me but none came.

I held onto my rage, my anger. It would spill over in venting and frustration and annoyance. I was angry at a lot of surface stuff. I was angry at stuff that didn't matter and I took everything personally.

That helped me stay away from people. It helped me push people away. It helped me live into and create the identity of the girl who didn't need anyone. It helped me grow into the person who screwed people before they screwed me.

It helped me say no to dates and play hard to get. It helped me crush guys and treat them like crap. It helped me stay silent and not be "that girl" who shared too much, who shared her shame stories and it helped me be someone I was not, someone I thought was better, someone I thought people would like more, would fit in more, and someone who didn't care if I didn't.

I never said what really mattered. I never spoke from my heart. In fact, I got off on pretending I didn't have a heart.

Chapter Twenty-Two

BE

t's easy to see how others show up or don't show up. It's easy to see what they do, how they do it. And it's easy to judge every gesture, every comment and take it all personally. It's easy to look for the bad in person, the wrong they do.

It's far easier to hold on to pain for fear we might end up hurt, alone, weak, scared, and vulnerable. It's easier to put up walls and hide behind them then it is to stand out and stand alone.

It's easier to hide who we are and what happened to us than it is to show our scars. Because if we hide ourselves and our true stories then we can know inside of us that we protected ourselves, we never put ourselves out there, we never tried and so no one can reject us if we don't try.

It's easier to hold onto the knife by the blade. And it's easier to change who we are, to conform, to get the rewards dished out to us by a society who is comfortable not seeing things that make us uncomfortable. We want to turn a blind eye to suffering because it keeps us from changing, from having to face it, from having to look right at it.

I kept my mouth shut because I didn't want to make other people uncomfortable. I didn't want to be the broken, damaged girl. I didn't want that to be my story. I wanted to be like the other girls who didn't have this crap in their lives.

When I finally started speaking about my abuse I realized that I was normal. 1 in 4 is a joke. The numbers of harassments, abuse, rape, molestation, violations, threat of it keep women nodding and smiling, keeps them in their place.

I always wanted to be normal, to not have this gaping hole in my life. When I realized I was normal because of what happened, I was sad and while I didn't want to have this in common with so many other women, I recognized the camaraderie we shared, the knowledge, the understanding of what we have experienced.

I didn't want to be loved for who I was, I wanted to be loved for being whole, for being normal, for being someone who did not have a giant shame story.

It's easy to become the person who laughs, jokes or even complains about the stuff than it is to be who you are. Because when we are who we are without any walls, any protection we are open to the rejection that we will not be enough for someone.

But I've learned we will also be too much for others. Some people will manipulate and control and try to blame you when they are caught out, they will go for your weak spots and when you're living in fear and behind walls and don't know who you are, it's easy to fall for those things.

Some people give to get. They don't give to give. When giving has strings attached it's not coming from true contribution, it's coming from trading something—you are indebted to them.

"Look what I did for you." When we keep score or to get something that's not coming from contribution, it's coming from control (certainty) and Importance (significance). We have all done this to others and we've all had it done to us.

I've had plenty of it done to me—the giving me something but wanting something in return. Or the withholding of something that was intended to make me conform.

When people play games like this it's damaging to all people involved. They play coy with the truth. They pretend they weren't playing games. And it harms the relationships. We learn not to trust people's motives and if they can convince us we were wrong, we learn not to trust ourselves, our own intuition, our own knowing.

We lose the connection with ourselves. Because the truth is not something we value. We value lies, we value pretending and acting like everything is ok.

I never actually felt that I wanted to be loved for who I was. I always believed there was something wrong with me. I played the trade game too—become what they wanted, go along with to get approval, love, connection, significance. We can't only see what others did to us, that is the victim in us. We have to look at how we show up too, how playing the games meets our own needs in some way.

I traded my voice for security, safety, and certainty. I traded my voice for financial rewards. I dulled who I was and what I really needed and wanted to say because I was afraid I'd offend people, especially clients, and I was afraid they wouldn't work with me.

I traded sex for significance. I traded myself to be safe. I gave myself up, I traded who I was and what I believed in to fit, to blend and to not make others uncomfortable.

We all trade things until we realize what we're doing, that we're selling out, selling our soul to meet our needs in some way.

For eons women have learned to trade, to silence, to put up or be blamed. We've learned that it's always our fault—what we wore, where we went, how we behaved, the vibe we put off. I hear far too many stories of women who put out because it was better than being raped.

I know too many women who did it because it was their only option—they were in a situation where they were scared and felt it was the only thing to do. They wouldn't dare tell anyone because they would be blamed and publicly shamed.

So, we learn to say nothing, we accept the blame, we blame ourselves and we shove it away, into the black whole. Looking back on who I used to be, I honestly can't say what I felt. I didn't feel at all. I think I just knew this was how it was. I had forgotten that I had changed who I was and that change was to fit in, to be normal, to be liked, to avoid seeing this gaping hole in my life.

The filters through which I was living changed, so did my values and beliefs. I couldn't not see how I was showing up, what I was tolerating and choosing for various reasons. I had a choice but I didn't feel like I did. I didn't have to play the game this way. But I did because I valued myself so little, I saw myself as being broken, something wrong with me, and running from my story.

I was so busy being perfect and looking away from things I didn't see that perfection was the very thing robbing me of a life. I didn't see that running from my story; my inability to own my story was the thing that kept me imprisoned.

Finding who we are is one thing, being it is another. It's not easy to suddenly start being yourself when you've acted another way your entire life.

Being ourselves can only happen when we're willing to show up, to fight, to connect, to lay it all out on the line. The more I started realized just how much I silenced myself, how much I traded myself, I was done with being polite and nice.

I was here to be real, to speak the truth, to say what I meant and mean what I said. I wasn't here to be some ornament but that's how I acted my entire life. Nothing I did mattered if it wasn't shrouded in the ability to look a certain way, to have sex appeal, to be wanted.

The more of this behavior I witnessed within myself, the more sickened I became of who I had become, how I sold myself for something. I was done trading my integrity, my respect and my value for a quick fix. I was done trading my self respect for a knowing look—satisfying my ego.

There is a huge difference in being wanted and being valued. And I was learning the difference and learning how to stand up for myself. Instead of being the non-demanding girl, not like the other girls who were demanding and jealous or offended by everything, I allowed my respect to be rolled out and walked on in an effort to be the girl who could roll with the boys.

Having lunch with one of my male friends one day while he snapped his head and ogled the passing women showed me how little I stood up for myself and my fellow sisters.

I told myself for years that women were too sensitive. But sitting there watching him ogle the girls made me feel sick. I realized just how disrespectful this person was to women and I didn't want to be around it.

As I paid attention to his behavior I saw that his version of loving women was not how women wanted to be loved. We don't want to be objectified, not really.

I did. For most of my life I wanted to be objectified as a measure of my worth, my value. I used to ask *but would you pick me up and do me*? I cringe at those memories and what that said about how little I valued myself.

The more of this stuff that emerged, the more I stood up and said no, I wanted something more for my life. Yes, I want to have a healthy fit body, yes, I want to look good—but not for a one-night stand as a measure of who I am, but because my body is the vehicle in which I experience life and I want it to be as healthy possible—not as an indicator of worthiness to tell me that I'm good enough.

Because it doesn't tell me I'm good enough. It tells me I'm broken. It tells me I have self-esteem issues and it tells me I have no idea who I am or what I'm worth.

As the singer Pink said, *when you know what respect is you'll realize it tastes so much better than attention.* My body was my value; that overshadowed everything else.

As I realized how I was showing up in my own life, the behavior I was accepting from people around me I began to stand up in a new way. I didn't giggle at stupid jokes. I didn't just take the crumbs that were handed to me. I didn't accept that I wasn't important, or wasn't as important as someone else.

I asked to be treated better. I asked for what I wanted. I stopped fixing everything like it was my fault. I stopped taking the blame for what wasn't mine to take. I stopped trying to make everyone else happy and stopped trying to prove myself. I focused on being happy for myself. I focused on seeing my own worth, seeing what I was good at and what kind of person I was.

I decided to be myself and like my own self. What if it was possible to like myself, to love myself, to see myself as a person of value, not because I had a hot body or because I went along with things but because I was a human being who deserved love and respect simply because I existed.

Each time I was faced with a situation in which to behave differently, I felt the terror, and many times I backed down, I went back to being safe, I went back to old patterns where it was easier to just give in and be what others expected and needed so they could be safe and comfortable.

My time in the fitness industry had come to an end. I knew the end was coming for a long time because I was now acutely aware that I had gone into the fitness industry because I wanted to teach what I had learned about our ability to create our own destiny. I had originally started this to deal with my eating disorder I felt the fitness industry was the place to do this work.

But this journey, the finding myself back with eating disorders and ending up on an epic spiritual and emotional journey taught me that there was far more to this than just for people who wanted to lose weight. Yes, I help people do that too, but even more profoundly I was helping people find themselves and be themselves.

In order to be myself and be who I was born to be, I had to be willing to give up the old way and the old way was focusing only on people who wanted to lose weight.

The more I was asked to step into this work, not just my own work but the work I was feeling called to do in teaching this to other women, in holding this space with other women in coaching, retreats and other venues, the more scared I became.

And the more fear I worked through the deeper layers or myself that I found. I felt called to be in this space with women and began hosting retreats, coaching sessions, workshops, speaking and just sharing my experiences and helping guide women on their own journeys.

And it was amazing, vulnerable, real, raw and honest. There was so much beauty in standing together with women who started to show up for themselves, to explore, to open their pain and let it flow out, to see them reclaim their spark, their joy and their openness, their real selves was something that set my own soul alight.

Watching women reclaim their fire stoked my inner fire at a deeper level.

But something began to shift the more I began to share. The more feedback I received, the negative comments, the sideways comments…I began to hold back, to hide a bit.

I wasn't truly able to be myself. I felt shame over this new world I had been exploring. Comments from people about, *"what I was into"* clearly said as though it was bad thing. Non-conformity isn't approved. You've got to have a good belief in yourself to be able to withstand the judgment that will come when you are doing anything outside the norm.

At first, I was feeling so powerful, so good, so open to building the new me, to BEING me for the first time ever. But the resistance set me back. The lack of approval and understanding set me back. The judgment set me back. And soon I found myself withdrawing. Closing off, protecting myself. I was being myself in safe places. I was being myself at events and with people I knew would understand. I wasn't being myself all the time, I was still fragmenting, I was still running from my story.

I had not fully owned my story. I wasn't filling the cracks with gold. I was still hiding them, still only talking about them in safe places.

I was still developing; still finding who I was and there were a lot of times it was too challenging. I dulled it down. I toned it down. I didn't write the things I wanted to. I felt stifled, suffocated again. I wanted to break free but I was too scared.

I heard what people said. I remembered how terrified of meditation I was! I wondered often what people thought of what I was writing, what I was saying and the photo's emerging from my retreats. Sometimes I wanted to delete people's comments and tags.

The safer I played it the more I lost me again. The more I worried. I worried about the impact it would have on my business. Would people want to work with me? Had I gone too far out there? Had I pushed too many people away? Am I too weird?

I felt the familiar pull of safety, letting fear lead the way. My shadow beckoning me closer, to be wrapped in her dark coils of protection where it was safe, where I could be normal, where I could forget all of this stuff and just get a job and go back to real life.

I felt at times caught in between two worlds—trying to be and trying to fit at the same times. I was still changing myself. I was still playing with the idea. Even though I was now teaching this I was still hiding in the closet, one foot in and one foot out.

What had caused this? I had felt so open and vulnerable and real and raw for a time. The freedom of that was still glowing inside of me but at times I was living in profound fear and judgment of the world I now played in. I could see I had retreated into the safety of half living again. Caught in the stories, caught in fear and playing small.

Why was I struggling so much with being? I was coaching people. I was now hosting regional, national and international retreats, was being published in online publications, getting radio and print interviews, had even written most of this book. But there, lurking in the shadows was the cold fingers of not enoughness, of fear telling me I couldn't do it, that I was crazy, what did people think? The voices of my critics drowned out the voice of my soul.

Should I be teaching this? The limiting beliefs were back. The negative voices telling me to give up, I wasn't good enough, I didn't have it together.

The issue now was I could feel when I was hiding. One upon a time I had no idea what authenticity was. Now I could feel the heaviness, the weight, the exhaustion, the frustration, the annoyance that happened when I was disconnected from my real self and living in defense and protection, when I was living in hiding.

I always had to fill the space, the cracks. I had to fill the pause so there was no room for me to be me in case I said something I shouldn't have.

And I didn't like it.

Chapter Twenty-Three

BLOCKED

What caused me to go back here? I had to know. My life's work is based on breaking patterns. I knew if I didn't find the root it would keep repeating itself. I had to find the cause, when I started to slip away again.

I knew it would be painful; it would lead me to some deep work that I wasn't sure I was ready for. But I could never go back to the old life and my new life was still calling, asking me to lean in, step up even more into this work.

I was unable to write, feeling blocked. I was judging people, separating myself from people, pushing people away. What had happened? I was living in frustration; annoyance and I was most certainly not being who I really was.

I knew I was blocked so I went to my shaman for an energy clearing. I hadn't been doing many because I had been doing so well. But clearly, I had slipped and didn't see it. Getting to the root of it was going to require a good energy session to stir up and unblock the energy so I could see it.

After, as I began to write, calling on jaguar, I felt the flow of the hurt I had stored and started carrying. I had been stepping out. I was being more of who I knew myself to be. And I had an incident with a friend where I felt taken advantage of, unseen, unimportant. I felt pushed aside.

I didn't stand up for myself. I got angry, I vented, I complained. But I never addressed it. I never spoke up; I never had a conversation; I stuffed it all back down.

Old patterns had emerged. The lack of taking divine action had reared its head. I couldn't skip step 5 in my process forever because nothing would change if nothing changed.

But I did skip it. I brushed it away. Said she wouldn't understand. It was pointless—the most common phrase I used to silence myself. Instead of addressing anything I would tell myself it was pointless—they wouldn't see my point of view. I would look bad, petty and it would impact our friendship.

A few weeks later my dog, Tetley, was hit by a car. The person who hit her sideswiped her. We were walking our normal morning route when she bounced across the street away from me. The car was coming so fast I didn't have time to react. She went off the road and side swiped Tetley, breaking her hip and sending her flying through the air. A moment I'm not sure I'll ever recover from.

At the time I decided that bad things happen and sometimes we don't know why it happens but we need to deal as best we can, choose our battles and move forward.

I blamed myself. And while she went off the road and blamed Tetley for running in front of her, I couldn't physically bring myself to go to that person and say anything. I let it go. That was the start of my silencing myself. With my friend a few weeks before and now this. The swallowing down had begun, to not rock the boat, not address things.

Fatigue set in. I blamed it on Tetley's accident. I wasn't sleeping. I was tired. I started drinking more coffee and while I had not been using food or cigarettes in more than 2 years, I did start eating oddly again. Not quite abusing food but I began to notice I wasn't dealing with things as well, I wasn't writing as much and I was eating more of my feelings.

I could see it but I wasn't quite in it, the disconnect had surfaced. I wasn't looking right at it. The old coping skill of seeing what I wanted to had come back. I kept saying I'd get back to it. I had become quite busy with business, international retreats and this new "role" I had taken on as I transitioned the business with my own life. I was busy....

And in that busy I wasn't being. Things started happening with people that I needed to address but I had lost my voice again. I started pushing stuff away again and convinced myself these things didn't matter.

But they did matter. There were things that were disrespectful, rude, crossing boundaries that I just let go. The lines became blurred until there were no lines anymore.

Fatigue is the first sign for me that I'm storing things. But with lacking sleep after Tetley's accident, it was easy to miss that. It was easy to misdiagnose it. It was easy to revert as the old safety and protection called me back.

Don't rock the boat. Don't jeopardize anything. I was trading my voice, myself for something else. I didn't know what though. What was

I scared of? What was drawing me back to this place of fear? Why was I so scared to act? Why was I so scared?

Why was I so scared?

Chapter Twenty-Four

REACT

sat bolt upright in bed in the cottage we were staying at in Twillingate. I could feel unhappiness had set in again. I had gone along with plans I didn't want to go along with. I didn't want to force the issue. I was scared he'd be mad. At least that's what I tell myself. But these last few years I hadn't been scared? So, was this really true or was the issue that I was pushing it all down again and festering? So why was I unable to do that now? What was stopping me from speaking up? Was this a convenient story I was telling myself to help me withdraw and put walls up?

What was the truth? I could sense a fracture in how I was seeing things.

With him, with friends, with clients, with other people—why did I become too scared to speak up and withdraw into myself? When this happened, I became angry, bitter, frustrated, I noticed all the flaws and none of the good…and then seeing myself this way…I questioned my ability.

Then the limiting beliefs would return. The ways I held myself back—I'm not ready. Look at me, what right do I have to teach anything to anyone else? I can't do this. It won't work.

At the root—no one cares.

My go to phrase—no one cares. No one cares about me. No one cares about themselves. No one cares. This is one of my core beliefs—that no one cares about me.

Was it really things that were happening that were the problem or was there more to it? Things were getting confusing—which they always do when we find ourselves in conflict with our beliefs and perceptions.

I was seeing something that didn't make sense. And I realized it was my reactions not the actual things themselves that were the problem.

Because in every case I had a choice but I never felt like I could choose. I would internalize almost immediately. Instead of being able to express myself in the moment, I got angry and withdrew. Then I'd stay there for as long as it took for me to get exhausted from being angry and upset.

Something would happen, what though? I didn't know exactly what was causing this to happen. But I knew my response wasn't intentional, it wasn't planned and I didn't see it for what it was.

I saw it as what they did to me. I saw the problem as their behavior and I was a scared little child, too afraid to stand up for myself, so I'd withdrew into myself.

The world shook a little as it always does when I uncover something like this. This wasn't a small thing I knew it. I felt it. In fact, I felt it so intensely that I knew everything had been leading me here.

This was a plate shifting earth shattering something…BUT WHAT? Why couldn't I see this?

As I sat bolt upright that morning in the cottage I went to my journal, sat on the couch with Tetley, my feet under her warm body as I looked at my blank page and wrote *"what am I scared of. I'm always terrified. I physically cannot stand up for myself. Then I react by shutting down because I'm not being heard"*. And the memories of the past year washed over me. While it had been spectacular and amazing, it was also one of the most challenging.

Fear steals more dreams than failure ever will. Fear will destroy you and your dreams if you don't get in the ring with it.

When we ask a question; the universe will help us find the answer. When we set goals, the universe will help us clear the blocks that are in the way of those goals. When we get on our path, the universe will clear the way. That clearing is not usually filled with unicorns and butterflies.

I had big goals and in order to achieve them I had to show up as the best version of myself. In order to go where I wanted to go, this behavior of shutting down had to stop. I had to stop censoring myself. I had to stop shutting myself down. I had to stop withdrawing into a world where no one could reach me.

Chapter Twenty-Five

CLEANSE

During a Wild Soul Women retreat I was hosting in Costa Rica, I invited my shaman to join us. As this was my first International Retreat it felt safe and comforting to have a mentor, someone who could provide the stability and insight, guidance and help should I need it and also add some ceremonies and her special touch to my retreats.

During one of our evening experiences, she took us on a journey. Her ability to make you literally experience these things while feeling safe in on your yoga mat was truly amazing. Journeying isn't like meditation, not like guiding. When journeying is fully experienced it's as if you're really doing it, you can smell, taste and feel and even have memory recall as if you really did it. Well, as the shamans would say—you DID do it!

We journeyed with the whales from Canada all the way to Costa Rica. As we took this journey I was feeling amazing but then I began to feel fear, immense fear. My whale told me that I had to release this fear if I was going to be able to live my life.

I had to find the source of the fear so I could defeat it. I had to understand this and let it go. I was easily malleable, too naïve and despite being very intuitive I wasn't seeing clearly. I had to find the source of this fear so it wasn't controlling me. Because this fear was causing me to see and perceive things differently than they were. I was processing them through fear.

I was living into a very negative belief system. Setting myself up for International women's retreats was very difficult, everything inside of me was challenged and I wasn't growing through it well. I was living in fear, I was complaining; seeing the negative and playing into it.

I could see myself doing it and knew I had to shift but I could not seem to. I played out the negativity and judgement over and over. I began to see behaviors I had not had in a very long time re-emerge and I wasn't in a good vibing space.

During this meditative journey I was thrown on the beach by the whale who spoke to me, telling me it was time to look deeper at this pattern because it was a reoccurring theme in my life and that I knew it wasn't about what people did but it was about my perception of it and what I made it mean.

The whale said *you know this. You are strong enough to do this. It's just another, deeper layer on the journey, these will come for your lifetime as long as you are on the shaman's path, the medicine woman's path, the sage's path. As long as you are committed to this work, there will be down moments, peeling back the layers moments, diving deep moments. They won't be as hard to get to and you won't stay as deep but don't think because you are a teacher that you don't do this work, don't work through deeper layers. You are not a failure for this, you are in fact, committed to greatness and you live what you teach"*.

In the journey, when I landed on the beach my head split open and it lay there in 2 complete pieces. Millions of spiders started coming out—they were marching out. I was terrified, horrified at the same that I felt in awe. It was like watching soldiers marching. As I watched them I wanted to understand what they meant, what they represented to me and I realized they were the toxic thoughts that I was having. The seeds planted by myself and others and tended and watered by myself. I grew a garden of toxicity, cultivated in fear.

This wasn't my first encounter with spiders during mediation. During a recent visit with my shaman—before this Costa Rica trip—I was releasing some stress and pressure for the upcoming retreat. As I was about to lay back on her bed I felt something crawling out of my eye. It wasn't actually there but it felt real. I was startled by it and tried to get up. But she nudged me down, and I felt this giant black widow spider crawl out of my eye. I was aware of the vacant space in my head and the spider just hovering above. As we proceeded with the healing release, the spider got smaller and smaller until it disappeared. Later I looked up the significance of a black widow and I was told it was a toxic relationship I was in with someone.

As I lay on the floor of the yoga shala in Costa Rica, I knew the millions of spiders marching out were the millions of negative thoughts, the dark clouds, the seeds planted and the remnants of the black widow. And I knew there were several people in my life that represented the black widow and that I would need to step back from those people. On the surface it was hard because we can fool ourselves into thinking people are good for us because everyone else loves them, they have the right charm and charisma, and it's easy when you live a life of doubting yourself, to think it's you and not them.

But I learned to listen to my instincts, my gut, from numerous failures to do so, that energy and instincts don't lie and someone doesn't have to be a bad person to be not right for you.

There was so much fear, fear of disappointing people, fear of being myself, fear of fear itself and all of those spiders represented that fear, all of those fears. The fear had begun taking over when I began silencing myself, with Tetley, with friends, within my business…the silencing, the stuffing down was the key to the next puzzle piece.

I reflected on the question that I woke up with "what am I afraid of"? as I recalled the spiders and Costa Rica and the whale journey as I was looking out the window of the cabin in Twillingate with Tetley by my side I knew there was something big here—something that had changed me forever.

It was time to face my fears and move to a new level of healing—to understand why I had created this pattern again. Why was I being so negative, so reactive to things? What was going on? What was it I needed to learn that was preventing me from being who I really was?

Since I've always been terrified of spiders it was a big notice that I was holding onto a fear and that it was time to explore it and release it.

I began the search for the answers. I was shrouded in confusion. And I knew confusion meant a breakthrough was coming. I kept asking, kept praying for the answer, kept using my tools but I couldn't get a good connection to anything.

I felt blocked. I couldn't meditate. I was struggling to breathe. I had a lung problem develop where I was shallow breathing. I know our emotional blocks show up in the body so I was trying to find the solutions but this one was resisting me. Nothing was getting me closer.

In an effort to find the answer without my shaman, she travels a lot and wasn't available, I decided to visit the John of God bed, which is a crystal healing bed owned by a woman that I had coincidentally met when I ran my fitness business and now we were both finding ourselves in this new, deeply spiritual world. I was feeling angry and stuck in the story of who had done what to me, again. While part of me knew I had to let this go, part of me was holding onto it. That was part that wanted to scream, *see, this is why I locked you up*! because you're an idiot for trusting people and expecting them to treat you better.

As I lay on the bed, the operator placed a headset over my ears and drums filled my space. Drums bring me to another world instantly. As I was lying on the bed I called on my guides and animals to help me, to guide me.

And just like that I was gone. I felt as though I were free falling and I landed with a thud in front of a medicine man. Not my shamanic healer, this one was a Native American Shaman. He was old and wrinkly. He had warrior paint on his face. I noticed my jaguar was with me.

He helps me leave my body behind to take these journey's knowing my body is safe and protected and that he will wake me if I should be in danger. And he helps me experience things.

The medicine man invited me to follow him along a path. As we walked we began to hear drums and I noticed a clearing up ahead. I wanted to enter the clearing but he stopped me. He indicated I needed to clear myself before I could enter. He sage me; clearing my energy field and the energy field of my jaguar. He then asked me to howl. I was taken aback. I didn't understand why he wanted me to do this.

He told me my throat chakra needed clearing. It was not operating properly. I wailed for what seemed like forever. Each time I'd stop and try to enter the clearing, he would stop me. And finally, I threw back my head and howled until I was exhausted, until there was nothing left.

Opening my eyes, he welcomed me to into the clearing where a group had gathered together; I was the special guest. Suddenly I was thrown into the circle, landing face down. I was scared, trying to get up but I realized I had turned into a baby.

My jaguar was pacing the circle. A woman stepped forward. She appeared to be a mother Theresa energy, a mother Mary, a divine mother energy. She reached out to pick me up. I was scared. I didn't know what she wanted and I was too little, I couldn't defend myself, I couldn't't stop her.

She held me. She stared into my eyes and I struggled, screaming, crying and wailing. I wanted to be let go. I didn't like this. I fought it. But she held tight. She was pouring love into me. I couldn't resist it anymore. As she did, I was moved to tears. In the circle I was giggling and cooing as a baby would but in real life on the bed, tears were steaming down my face as I felt the most powerful love I had ever felt.

I felt I was being given unconditional love for the first time in my life. I had never felt this before. I had never felt unconditional love. I knew only conditional love—behave and you'll get approval and praise. Be "bad" and you'll get punished. The definition of bad was always changing. Sometimes bad was just being myself.

As I embraced this love and let it pour into my heart, I felt myself relaxing and opening. Mother hugged me and she passed me to the next person and the next. Around the circle I went and I was passed around I was growing up, getting bigger. As I was about to be handed to an uncle figure I became scared and nervous. I didn't know what he would do.

But he tossed me in the air and played with me. As I was handed around this circle of my metaphorical, spiritual family I began to feel healed, as though there was nothing wrong with me.

Landing once again with a thump in front of the medicine man, he was smiling. He wanted me to have fun he said. I had become too serious. I had lost my way but was on the right path. I asked him if he knew what had happened. Why had I reverted a little and he replied that it was all part of the plan. I wasn't off course at all.

He reminded me that we can only learn in bits. It's too much. We must learn, integrate, grow, fall and repeat these cycles until we become who we really are.

I understood. This was all part of a bigger plan to help me reclaim an even deeper part of me. As we spoke I was transformed into a warrior goddess. The medicine man told me I had to take the next journey alone. He gestured to a doorway.

My jaguar and I approached the door. I looked back at my new spirit family. I didn't want to leave. I didn't know what was on the other side of the door. I was scared. What if I went through it and I started a free fall?

What if I lost my mind and I couldn't function anymore? What if I went too far into this and I was bible thumping, robe wearing weirdo? These are the thoughts that went through my mind. Hand on the knob I was trembling. I couldn't do it. This field was beautiful. Why couldn't we stay here?

Jaguar nudged me forward. The look in his eyes told me I needed to trust this process, trust him to help me, that he wouldn't lead me astray. I turned the knob and we stepped through, stumbling into a field exactly like the one we had just left.

I turned around but the doorway had vanished. Jaguar shrugged reminding me I was afraid of nothing. I had a big bad wolf story made up in my mind. I was scared of free falling into nothingness but here I was feet on the ground just on the other side of the door.

I got the lesson. Stop making up stories about what could go wrong and start realizing what could go right. Trust.

We set out on our journey. I had no idea where were we going or what the purpose was. We just had fun along the way. I was excited to be the warrior goddess leaping and jumping through the forest. We came to a high mountaintop, overlooking a Sahara of sorts. It was desert landscape.

As we admired the view, we could feel the ground rumbling and, in the distance, we could see the dirt rising. Approaching us was thousands of animals. I stood in awe as they stopped in front of me below the mountain. Jaguar and I stood staring at them. I had seen this vision before.

In one of my healing sessions I had seen this exact scene before me as the animals had shown up. It's no surprise to me that animal medicine is so powerful for me because I have always profoundly been drawn to animals.

It's why I cannot eat them. I feel their suffering. I feel what they felt.

As we headed down the mountain we joined the animals—there were thousands of them—jaguars, elephants, lions, giraffe's, wolfs, so many animals as far as I could.

We continued on our journey. There was somewhere we had to be although I didn't know where. The animals followed us. I was leading with thousands of animals following me.

As I neared the edge of another mountaintop I could see a figure ahead of me. I slowed my pace. It was a man, dressed in what I would have believed God to look like. As I slowed, he beckoned me. I was hesitant but as I approached he pulled no punches.

You have forgotten who you are. You weren't born to fit in. If you did you couldn't change the things you're here to change. You don't want to rock the boat, but warrior; you were born to do that very thing. It's time to rock it. It's time to stop playing games and claim your destiny. Stop talking to fools. You're dabbling. You're going to everyone to find the problem. You know the answer is inside of you. No one else can answer it and you're spreading yourself everywhere, talking to people who know nothing about your journey or your purpose. You were given the heart of a warrior. It's time to be who you were born to be. You have access to everything I have [And he spread his arms to the world in front of us, including the animals]. You just have to ask. It's time to claim and live your destiny. And that's isn't playing small or safe. It owns all of you and claiming all parts of you. You're here to rock the boat and challenge people to see things a new way. You're here to be warrior. Now go be one.

And he put war paint on me. Under my eyes and he tied a band around my arm. And suddenly I landed with a thump in front of my medicine man again. I told him of my experience and he invited me to train. I had free will so I did not have to take this role.

As I looked into his eyes I could see my destiny. I could see I was born to do this. This was who I was—the warrior. I might have been a wounded one, I might have gotten lost along the path but now I was here to reclaim who I was.

La Loba—the bone collector—warrior goddess—the breather of souls back into the body. First the journey was mine to take, now it's mine to give away.

I was presented with a sword and I recognized this image too from another meditation where I saw a guide holding a sword with his head bowed. I thought it was a sign that I was being protected by him but I suddenly realized he had been offering it to me. I could choose to pick up my sword and fight or I could stay a victim.

I chose the sword. And was shown how to use it and we underwent training. I was given a celebration of warrior goddess status. My tribal family honored me. It was time to leave. My medicine man walked my Jaguar and I to the clearing. He reminded me that he was at the fire every day and I could join him anytime to talk by taking a journey.

He reminded me this was my time. It was time to reclaim who I am and step into the world to fulfill my destiny.

Being myself meant I had to reclaim all parts of myself—not just sometimes, not just when I felt safe, but the only way to be me was to fully own all of who I am, that meant bringing back and owning the stories of what made me who I am.

If I was going to fulfill my destiny I had to let go of this withdrawing and hiding and playing safe. I had to stop dilly-dallying. I had to step up and BE WHO I WAS.

My constant search to be enough, give enough, do enough was still exposed and there was only one way to fill the emptiness inside of me—that was to decide that I was good enough, that my stories weren't something to be ashamed of and that I was here to be the warrior, to rock the boat and have the tough conversations.

I wasn't here to make nice or placate people. I wasn't here to let people wear rose colored glasses and that meant I had to become ok with my role because such a role means I could be abrasive to people, I will touch up against people's wounds, their belief systems and I won't always be saying things people want to hear.

I had to move into a head and heart space where I could do that, where I could be the person who could hold that space and the only way I could was to bring all parts of myself back.

I couldn't play it safe by being me in safe situations only. I had to stop hiding and I had to accept my path, my purpose and my life as it was unfolding.

I was still resisting it, still wanting it to be something more normal, more mainstream, more accepted. I know that a lot of what I do and talk about isn't yet what people are ready to hear, to see or know. I know I am into things that many people in my life don't understand and will say there's something wrong with me because I'm doing it.

And worst, they may reject me entirely for me being me, even in the telling of these stories, this journey, these experiences, there is a fear of the unknown of what people will think.

I had to be willing to accept that and accept that anyone who rejects me for being me isn't my tribe, they aren't my people. And that meant it was time to fully own myself, my shame stories and all the broken parts of me that I felt were holding me back, the things I still didn't want to own or tell people or have people know about me in a way that I wasn't ready for or in a way that I couldn't control the details.

I was terrified of letting go, of becoming ungrounded. And I was scared of something else too, something I couldn't quite name but was sitting inside of me keeping me in the dark, keeping me in hiding, something I could feel in my body but I could not seem to find or see.

But the time was now. It was time to do this, to step into this. I was no longer in the space of being able to play the small game. I had been awakening to a new path and the universe was calling me.

The wild had put her call out to me, again, to grow deeper, to come home even more, to let go and surrender into this.

Chapter Twenty-Six

RECLAIM

We reclaim ourselves, we have to break down all the parts of us that aren't us. Finding ourselves is less about finding us and more about unbecoming all that is not really us so we can be who we are. It's about breaking down the walls and rebuilding our lives.

It's letting the house that we've built to hide in crumble down around us and letting ourselves be exposed.

Vulnerability is our biggest fear. Being challenged to allow ourselves to be exposed—all of our secrets, all of our wounds out there on the table where people can see them is scary. We want to still control the conversation, to tell our own version or brush it away as not important.

We don't want to be uncomfortable in that space. We say that we need to destigmatize and that we need to talk about things but there is so much fear of doing it.

Reclaiming all of who we are is not a one-sweep process, although that would be nicer, it's not how it works. We fall because there is something we lost in the darkness, some part of us we left behind. Each time we dip down, peel another layer of the onion, it's to get that missing piece that we're now ready to bring back, that we now need.

The first time I did a soul retrieval was shortly after my date with destiny experience of finding myself locked away in the bird cage. I had become deeply aware that I was not being me but I didn't know how to be me, how could I bring her back into my life? I wasn't 10 anymore and I had no idea where to start.

My shaman took me through many soul retrieval processes—where she journeyed on behalf to find answers. I always slept during the process, during one particular one after I returned home from DWD, she shared her experience. Her version of finding the original wound was exactly the same as my experience at DWD. I was floored. I hadn't told her the details. Even though I had been seeing all of the synchronicities of this work and seen so many things happen that didn't make sense to the logic mind I was still a bit of a skeptic. I still held back from sinking into it.

But the experience had taken me through the process of what the wound was, why it was created, what contract I had made and what gifts I had before the contract and what part of me was ready to come back.

Contracts in the shamanic world are like decisions in my world. Metaphorically representing deeper truths that lay in our psyche's that haven't been uncovered.

I had decided when I was 10 years old that I wasn't good enough and that I was broken and I had better become someone tougher, someone who could not be impacted or hurt so easily.

I had made that decision from the space of my hurt, my abuse, my pain of rejection by friends and family. The gift I brought back that day was hope. I always had hope as a child.

Each time we experience a deep wounding we experience a rejection of a part of ourselves—a soul loss—that will profoundly impact us because of the decisions we make. In the shamanic world, there's a lot of symbolism and we have to find the messages of the animals, the guides, the contracts, the experiences that caused this and we have to find the beauty, the gifts in it.

As I began to nature my inner child and see through a lens of hope, I was able to bring parts of myself back. When I would feel anxiety and wanting to run away, to give up, to go back into hiding I would sit quietly and listen for what I was really feeling.

What was this trying to tell me? I was feeling unsafe, exposed most of those times. I was fearful of what others would think, fearful of being rejected and hurt and made fun of.

Unimportant. Railroaded.

Now I was able to parent myself into growing through this. I was able to remind myself I wasn't a child anymore and if people made fun of it or didn't understand me it didn't mean I was wrong. But I had a history of changing myself to fit in.

This process takes time—the reconditioning of our beliefs and fears that lead us to change who we are, to reject parts of us as not good enough, weird or strange and not accepting.

Through the work I was doing, it was increasingly clear that I had rejected any part of myself that was going to appear weak. Weak wasn't something I did well. Even my career in fitness was about strength.

Growing into the person we are requires us to bring back all that we are. And that means throwing off the shame, throwing off the belief that there is something wrong us, throwing off the fear of failure and rejection.

The privilege of a lifetime is getting to be who you are. That quote was given to me by my first business coach. It stayed with me, as though it spoke to a part of my soul that had not yet awakened but wanted to.

To do that we have to drop the masks, face it all, what's not working, how we have been showing up, what we're tolerating, what behaviors we're engaging in that aren't in our highest good.

We all have life conditioning, we all have inherited trauma and fear and many of us have trauma in our early lives that be explored.

Without trauma it might be easier to navigate but it's still challenging. I've been fortunate enough to work with people who have experienced all forms of trauma and people who have had no major trauma. And the challenges are similar.

The trauma survivors have extra and deeper layers, some more stuff to work through because of this but it's still a complicated world out there as we all try our best to live a happy healthy life.

We're told what that is and we often find when we get there it's not at all what we thought it would be. Stuff doesn't fulfill us and playing small doesn't fulfill, living in fear and not going after what we want creates bitterness and unhappiness.

We don't go after our dreams to save ourselves disappointment but then one day we realize it was better to be disappointed and have tried than to never have tried at all.

After the warrior experience I knew profoundly who I was and who I am here to help and what I am here to do, but I still had this unanswered question, *what am I so afraid of?*

I travelled to my friend's wedding in the Czech Republic and while it was a great time I could feel myself not there. I wasn't myself. I was very triggered and struggling in a way I hadn't in a very long time. When I had gotten there I was very positive. What had happened in the span of a few days?

I had an unnerving experience while out exploring on my own, with a group of men. I felt unsafe as they crowded me, coming up against my body, pushing into me, coming too close. I couldn't breathe, I was struggling for air as my fear gripped its icy fingers into my gut.

I was alone, there was no one else on the street, just me and 5 construction workers. I knew they could overpower me. My panic set in and I pushed my way through them, praying that they would leave me alone. They did.

Later I was struggling to hold on to myself, but I was blindly triggered and instead of asking for help, I shoved it down and told myself to get on with it. Out for drinks later, I felt like I didn't belong. That old familiar feeling of being unwanted.

I felt the familiar slipping away. I started wishing the trip away. I just wanted to go home. I put on the old mask of who I used to be so things didn't impact me but I began staying to myself, withdrawing. I could see it but I also couldn't stop it. I was watching myself from outside of myself again. I wasn't in my life as the bars closed around me, my heart and my chest, my breathe shallow as I went through the motions fighting panic attacks and the need to run away but unable to leave, so I froze.

I had gone into protection mode. Defense mode. I don't need anyone and I don't care mode. I tried to come back out but I couldn't seem to shake it. And it bothered me. Because I was different now. This didn't feel good to be here, to be caught, stuck in this vortex, this place of not living, of hiding. I was acutely aware that I was here but I felt powerless to stop it.

I just felt terrified and I couldn't get out from under it, I couldn't ask for help, I felt like prey, trapped in a cage waiting to be slaughtered. I tried to shake it off for the sake of the party and managed to for the last few hours.

I felt like an a**hole, really. I was so closed. And I wanted to be open.

As I returned home I was possessed by the question—what am I so afraid of? Why do I slip away like that? How can I get control of this? I began to feel the fear in my body, physically; I was trembling, my entire body shaking over nothing. There was no actual danger but I seemed to be flight mode and I couldn't get out of it. The only thing I can tell you is it grips my throat with its steel fingers and I feel like the life is being choked out of me, sinking all the way down to my heart where I feel the bars slam shut and into my gut as I sink into powerlessness.

I had never seen it like this before. Typically, I'd be triggered for months, lost, gone before I even knew what happened. My reactions to things had always been intense, me pulling away, leaving. Now I felt like I had watched the trigger, watched the slipping away, I tried to catch it, but couldn't. The off switch I had. Normally my off button was activated instantly, unconsciously.

The question of fear was plaguing me for months. I didn't want to live like this anymore. I didn't want to be that person who couldn't be present, who couldn't stay, who was drowning and couldn't ask for help. One of my best friends' weddings and I couldn't be there. I didn't know where this fear was coming from but I decided I was going to find out and get over this and take my life and my power back.

I booked a call with a coach friend of mine to help me uncover the issue. As we talked we uncovered a deep fear of speaking up and asking for help that was traced back to my abuse and the day it all came out. Standing in my bedroom with my school bag in my right hand… frozen in time. I could see me there, 9 years old and too scared to open my mouth.

I believed it was my fault.

And I didn't say anything. I stood there frozen. I wanted everyone be quiet and stop yelling. I wanted it to stop, to go away. So, I lied. I lied until I was 32 years old when he died and I couldn't lie anymore.

That was what I was so scared of. Speaking up. It was a trigger to silence myself and send me back behind my walls.

Silencing myself was how I lost myself. As I had begun to find myself and express myself over the these last few years I had taken my walls down. I let too many in, I was too giving, too open, too trusting and I was reminded how easily people can tear us down when we invite them in. The worst kind of poison is the drops places in your tea by friends.

A few incidents with friends, some off comments, deliberate attacks, off handed client remarks, not processed, stuffed down, looked away from and I had started to silence myself, slowly but surely. The more I pushed it down, the more it manifested in walls, in hiding and the longer it was down, the more I struggled with getting it up.

And I could do all the steps of the first draft and the truth I wanted, but until I moved to a place of action with speaking up, moving into a place where I wasn't afraid to speak, I would be here, triggered by fear.

I had some people I had to address. Not from my past but from my present, people who were in my life where things needed to be addressed. As I prepared myself to address it I realized just how terrified I was.

Not a normal fear or upsetting someone or things not going well. I was quite literally terrified. I could finally see that this fear wasn't normal and I forced myself to address the situations that had been piling up.

Things I had continued to ignore, deny, look away from, the making comfortable again. And somehow, I found the courage to dig deep and go for it. Let the chips fall where they may I thought.

After some conversations, emails and letters, both business and personal, my body shook for 7 hours. The muscles in my back, ribs, shoulders, were sore for 4 days after. Dealing with the situation that was really a 1-2 on a scale of 10, but felt like a 100 showed me how scared I was of speaking up and addressing things. Of saying what I wanted and needed to say, even asking for help.

To actually address things. And it wasn't even anything big. These were minuscule things in reality.

I began to replay images of clients, business dealings, friends, and family in my mind where I had needed to speak up and address something or ask for help and I physically could not. My mouth wouldn't speak the words. I would just fade away and internalize. Especially help. I could not. I had promised myself, made a soul contract, a long time ago that I would never ever need anyone else.

My fear wasn't normal. It was terror.

Chapter Twenty-Seven

SPEAK

That phone call from my mother heralding my abuser's death, changed the course of my life. I had been living a lie. I knew I couldn't run anymore and, as I replaced the receiver, I wondered how I could. But I knew I couldn't explain away an uncle who I'd never mentioned.

The reckoning had come. It was time to dance with what had brung me.

I told myself my whole life this was a non-issue. I had shame, yes. But I didn't realize this was the thing that had caused me to disassociate and go into the space where I had spent most of my life.

It was the most significant issue still impacting my life because sexual abuse runs deeps. It impacts mind, body, soul. Of course, I was disassociating and checking out from life. It was my survival mechanism.

And of course, I was scared of speaking up. I had been traumatized after the abuse. I wasn't given a safe space to tell the truth. If someone had explained to me that it wasn't my fault, if they had made me safe, I might have told.

I was still reacting like a 9-year-old—refusing to say anything and going in the corner with my arms crossed and jaw set. It was easier to be mad and withdraw than it was to be vulnerable and say "I'm hurting".

Even after all the work I had done, after everything I had experienced, I was still scared to own it all, still scared to open up that wound, I was still scared to take that part of me back because I still believed there was something wrong with me because of it.

My trigger was fear itself. And feeling unimportant, unseen, unheard.

When I felt scared I slipped away to another place, a place where I had walls up and when I had walls up it didn't take long for passive aggressiveness to come out, pushing people away, withdrawing from people. It was a lifelong coping tool.

I could now see the dots connecting since I was 10 years old and I decided not to need anyone, to become someone they couldn't touch, someone they couldn't reject.

And I fell. I felt the floor open up and swallow me, I sank into the blackness, again. I wasn't deciding this. I had decided it as a child and I was still reacting to perceived rejection. When I was gone I felt encased in cellophane. I could see and feel things but I was muffled. I was trapped in a world of my own making, a safe place for me to retreat.

As I had spent time opening myself to people, opening my heart, my soul, showing my wounds and stepping out there, I was exposing myself to potential hurt. Now I could see it didn't have to be that—it was how I perceived it.

It was an auto response to end up there. I had conditioned myself so well to go there as a safety mechanism for survival that it was now my go to place—withdrawal and become her. Become that version of me that wasn't really me but was created to help me protect the real me.

It was my response to trauma and now certain people, personality types, and perception of things like rejection, being unimportant, unseen as well as fear itself, were my triggers.

I turned into a 9 year every time I had to speak up and my body was reacting to the intense fear, even though it didn't exist in reality, it was very real to me.

It was time to deal with this fear, this trauma and these triggers at a deeper level. It was time I work with people who knew and understood my trauma, specifically my childhood sexual abuse trauma.

I was approved to attend a sexual abuse survivor's retreat. The universe was putting me in the situation where I could learn what I needed to learn about my specific ordeal, where I could meet other people who has my experiences and I could learn from professionals who understood sexual abuse and the trauma it leaves us with.

This was a huge step in being me. I had spoken about it. People knew but it wasn't something totally out there. I still only told it in places where I felt safe, where I wanted to share it. I was still playing safe with it.

This retreat meant potentially digging up things I didn't want to deal with. It meant everyone automatically knowing the deepest secret I'd ever kept. I wasn't sure I was ready but I felt pulled to be there.

I showed up in Utah and headed into the mountains with 30 other women. To give you an idea of the magnitude of this—they host 30-40 women weekly. How big of a problem is childhood sexual abuse? You have to be childhood survivor to attend here because trauma impacts children very differently.

I didn't understand that so much about my reactions to people and situations was caused by trauma. I had always just blamed myself for being a bad person. And I could see even more that many spiritual and positive thinking people I had followed were reinforcing that if I couldn't change my behavior by thinking positive, then I was just a negative person.

But now I could see the science behind it. I wasn't a negative or bad person. I was a person who had experienced significant trauma. A stimulus occurs and my brain automatically goes into survival mode. The limbic system kicks in and I'm reverted to behaviors to cope—reactions.

I just thought I was weak, there was something wrong with me, I was a coward, that I couldn't "get this". And each time I had an experience that drove me back into that place, when I withdrew I also fell into the old pattern of self-hate. How could I teach this? Look at where I am, again. I wasn't trying to be perfect but I wanted to not be doing this, I wanted to be able to truly live my life, not just exist. I was tired of this pattern, this behavior.

Learning that I was freezing as my brain's response to trauma was a relief to me. I now knew this wasn't something I had been able to control so it wasn't really something I was choosing. It was a long-standing survival mechanism.

I stayed frozen for 30 years.

Chapter Twenty-Eight

CLAIM

ourage isn't easy in the moment, it's fear walking. It's the knowing that in order to get to the next level I had to slay the dragon at this one. Like a video game, to get to the princess I had to defeat the dragon, only I'm not a princess I'm a warrior and I was defeating my own demons.

Each time I dealt with something from that box of darkness I reclaimed a part of me. I found me and I brought her back bit-by-bit.

Reclaiming yourself is parenting yourself, giving yourself all that you need to grow up as the real you this time. It's giving yourself permission to ask, to know, to love, to be messy and not perfect and find who you are.

Could I have done things differently? No. Because I had no idea what I was doing. It was my first rodeo. And even looking back over the course of 5 fantastical years, I recognize there was nothing I could have done differently. I was doing the best I could in dealing with a lot of life experiences that are hard to deal with, especially after living in denial for decade.

Now I understand that trauma changed me. It was the hardest part of my journey to accept that. I never wanted to be different or impacted by it. I wanted to pretend I was still fine, still normal, despite what happened. And the moment I accepted I was forever changed by my experiences was finally when I became unchained.

I realized that my story isn't different; it's not special. But it's mine, it's what makes me, me. And there are times I will be challenged; I will be changed for the rest of my life. I can't go back and be the girl I was going to if it didn't happen. She doesn't exist. But I was acting as though it didn't matter.

But it did matter. It did change me. It changed my reaction and my response to things. It will continue to impact me throughout my life. I can't just put it in a box and be done with it. It was a 9-year trauma. Repeatedly, until I was a shell of a person.

Who I became as a result was not the real me. It was the me I felt I needed to be to put distance between it and me so I could be normal.

Owning that it changed me, that my life is different from it, that my brain is different because of it, was a great impact on me. Looking at all those moments of impact, those stored emotions, the things I did, the things I let other people do to me, the times I lay down, the times I rolled over—when I should have been breathing fire but my inner flame was doused—it was hard to see those things. It was hard to see the truth, to feel the vomit rising inside of me as I explored all that darkness, all the truth that I hadn't wanted to see.

Imagine watching a movie of your life but you're not in it, not experiencing it as the first person, you're experiencing as a witness. It broke my heart, over and over and over. And in the breaking of my heart, the poison seeped out, freeing me from the prison I had created, unlocking the cage door in which I had been living and allowing my soul to step back into my body.

Owning my story was the most freeing thing I had experienced out of all of the things I had done. And every single thing I had done and experienced was all to help me get to the place where I could face and accept that truth.

It was ugly and it was painful. I mean, even typing it, I can feel the ugliness of a girl who didn't know who she was, who was over domesticated, over conditioned, hated herself, looking for approval, love, validation in all the wrong places.

Watching yourself be hurt, abused, mistreated is a pain that is unexplainable, only those who have turned away from the truth and lived in complete denial, can understand that feeling. I hope you never have to do it. But if you do, I can promise you, you're stronger than you believe. If you've buried your truth, your life, your soul then I know the pain you will feel when that arrow gets pulled back and forces you to look into that darkness.

The abuse changed me. It seems so odd that was a newsflash to me. I know it should seem like an obvious connection. But when you're living in denial and pretending it didn't happen and that there's nothing different about you, it can be a big shock to undercover that truth.

But even more so is the truth that I'm not weaker for it. I'm stronger for it. I've been through things in this lifetime that would break most people. I put myself in situations where I didn't care about myself, my life, my well-being, my safety. I traded myself, my life, my soul, my body for safety, for connection, for love or what I thought was love. I had no idea what love really was.

I turned away from my intuition, my gut and I went back to places and people who treated me poorly. In the end, when we see it all laid out in front of us, the truth, the mess, the disaster, we have to ask ourselves, why we would do that?

And in the end, the only answer I had was that I changed myself. I lost myself. I had no esteem, respect, and eventually, no power. The breaks I saw as my downfall, my weakness. But those breaks were actually my super power. It was all in the perception of how I saw it. What I made it mean and not the world.

It was time to fill my cracks with gold. It was time to own my story and write the ending myself, not just pay it lip service but to truly own it all, all parts of me and if someone else was uncomfortable with it, it was their problem.

I realized that by owning my stories and owning all parts of me, it would help those in my life better know and understand me, better equipped to help me through the tough days. As long as I was pretending it wasn't an issue, no one could help me.

And I couldn't help myself.

I couldn't go back and be who I would have been if it hadn't happened but I could go forward and be the best me in spite of it happening.

Since owning that it changed me, I have not once disassociated. I understand that my fears of speaking up are just fear. When I feel the fear, I give myself the love and care I need to help me through it. And when I feel like I want to be angry and slip away, I remind myself that I am not 9 anymore and that I can speak up. I do have a choice and a voice.

And now, I'm using my voice for good. I realize my story of healing has the ability to help others heal. Many people are in therapy their whole lives trying to get well but they don't realize it's their own rejection of the parts of themselves they feel are broken, damaged or dirty, whatever our story is. Maybe it's not abuses, maybe it's bullying, death or another trauma. It doesn't matter. When we reject and send away parts of ourselves, we have to get to work bringing those parts back, to stop walking away from the stories that make us who we are in order to fully heal and fully be present in our lives.

Only then can we fully live.

Chapter Twenty-Nine

BLEED

The more I understand my trauma the more I am able to heal and the more I am able to control my reaction. I am able to understand that I am safe and have a hold, a handle on things that I've never been able to handle. I don't flee inside myself, hiding behind walls, hoping it will go away.

We can't slay what we can't see.

In order for us to reclaim ourselves we need to see all of it. You've got to stop pretending you're ok. If you're unhappy with your life too many days in a row then you've got to take a look under the hood.

It's necessary to feel it, to let it bleed, let it out so you can release the charge, release everything that you are feeling, all of the bombs you kept inside, all of the times you put up, shut up, didn't speak up or say what you wanted to say in the moment or who you became and how you reacted.

When we don't speak up in the moment for fear of rocking the boat, fear of angering someone else or hurting him or her, we allow it to continue and it turns us toxic. I spent my entire life shoving it all down. I could write volumes on the amount of times I was a doormat.

I never ever asked to be treated better, so I wasn't. I never set boundaries so people did whatever they wanted with and to me. I would envy people who could speak up and say "don't treat me that way" or stand up for themselves. And while part of me thought, I shouldn't have to be asked to be treated that way, the reality is, when people show you who they are believe them. Maya Angelo said that.

I didn't believe them. People showed me who they were and I got in bed with them anyway, became friends with them anyway.

As hard as it is sometimes to understand when you're in a dark place, it's not what someone else does or says, it's not what happens, it's your reaction to it that matters most.

The fall is an important step to our growth—like an arrow—we have to fall back to move forward. I had to experience it the way I did in order for me to be able to go to each step. Like an escalator—the stairs appear for us. We can't get to the next stair until we finish what we need to at each level.

We can't stop the storms; they will keep coming. We will be triggered, bad things will happen, life will happen and if we can stay present to the process we can truly be in the moment, we can understand in the bad that they too have their purpose.

Getting to be the best version of myself was only possible when I was willing to look closely at the worst versions of myself so I could see what the patterns were, what the behaviors that I didn't like were, what cycles were repeating.

For a long time, I felt I didn't have the right to tell this story, to share it. I believed I wasn't courageous back then so why should I be courageous now. Do I have a right to walk in and grab this story?

But I realized my story is important because I was the silencer in my own story. People believed me. I had the chance to speak up. But I chose silence. And I chose silence for another two decades. Not just about my abuse but about so much.

Did I choose it? Sort of. Constrained choice is a big thing. We have a choice but don't feel like we do because we're operating from an outdated belief system and old operating system.

We can't move forward without an upgrade.

Chapter Thirty

UPGRADE

The purpose of life is to live it. And living it means feeling it… not fake feeling it through one-night stands and tequila shots. The hardest part I had to reconcile was who I became, the choices I made and how much of myself and my life I lost because of this. The residual re trauma I put myself through because of my actions—seeing how I accepted so little, whatever crumbs were tossed my way. That was hard to see.

How I treated others because of my perception of what they did to me. I couldn't, in those moments, see my own reactions. The victim— just how deep that ran through my life.

When we release that which holds us back—and holding onto everything might be justified but it doesn't serve our highest potential or good—it serves a platter of victimhood, bitterness.

We can't hold onto the experiences and stories of who did what and soar. That doesn't mean ignore them or pretend or deny. We don't have to be nice about it. For too long we've been taught to be pleasing, to be nice, to lay down and roll over.

We can bare our teeth, protect our boundaries, and speak the uncomfortable truth when we need to. We don't have to make it all better or make it anything actually. It's not my responsibility to fix anyone, change anyone, be good, make it better or more comfortable for anyone.

When we don't speak the truth, when we brush away, take away, and enable we rob a person of their chance to heal, to go deep and to find themselves. That includes ourselves.

Most of us are enabling ourselves into a submission, into what will make it better, make it ok. But somethings in life cannot be made ok. They cannot be changed or painted into something they're not.

It is not my job to shield the heart, the eyes, the soul of others so they can stay in their slumber and pretend. In fact, it is my destiny, my duty, my power, to tear Band-Aids off, expose wounds, to expose the soul less lives of so many; dancing outside themselves and making better.

For that is *wild at heart*—the ability to see it and call it for what is, without needing to make it something else. It's the ability to sit in the crap, to be in it and see it for what it is, to feel it. To experience it. To hold it in its place until it bleeds out the truth and the pain that is held in it.

Sacred rage is part of the journey. It has its place to help burn away the years and decades and even centuries of stored and stuffed down truths. There is a time for the inner wild woman to come clawing out, kicking and screaming and smashing down all those things, moments, experiences, beliefs, that has been spoon fed to us.

The big bad wolf isn't so scary when you realize it's not a wolf that's chasing you but it's your own species, your own breed, the ones who are supposed to keep you safe, nurture you, care for you and love you.

That bubbling pot can cut the cords of the past, throw off the shackles and let the wild woman come bursting out from inside of you, where she's been buried, planted, gaining strength and getting stronger to help you break free.

But there comes a time when that rage must settle because it cannot help us build a powerful, vibrant life. It is a step on the journey and once that step is complete we can move into a new phase of lightness, of hope, of creating from believing and being in our power.

When women call back their own power, remember they are wild, instinctual, capable, worthy, important, we are like wolves. We enforce our boundaries. We stand our ground. We go to battle. We hunt. We prowl. We play. We mother. We teach. We love. We roll over.

But we never lose our wildness, again. For when we have reclaimed her, and she is integrated within us, it can look like we've relaxed, let our guard down, and we can, for a moment, seem like prey again.

But in the moment of attack, of the words spoken, the action too far, the disrespect, the wild one emerges, eyes flashing, soul charged, teeth bared, instincts flared as she bares her teeth, reminding who she is.

The woman you become on the journey home to your own wildness will cost you the woman you used to be. I used to love being the damsel in distress, the demure, the savable, the needy one. That's what I thought I was supposed to be.

Shifting this perspective was the key to changing my relationship. I didn't understand us. I wanted one thing but acted like I was ok with something else, even said I didn't want the things I wanted.

I went along with, changed myself, became in an effort to be enough, pleasing and to fit what I thought he wanted. The changing back to myself, the reclaiming lost parts of myself meant I wasn't that girl anymore. I wasn't going along with, not asking for what I wanted or needed, not pining away in the corner waiting, hoping....

And it created a war zone for a time, angry, lashing out, frustration, silent treatment and a whole lot of deep breathing and holding on. I changed the rules of the game without telling him. I changed myself and said "hey, the girl you knew, she's gone".

So, I gave him time to catch up, to meet me where I was. I gave him time to adjust to the new world, the new life that we were both now living. I tore off both of our masks and shoved all of our stuff into the middle of the floor. I stopped sugar coating and painting it to over.

And I knew that it would work itself out. Either we be stronger and make it or we wouldn't. And I had to be ok with that. I had to be ok with the fact that if weren't living authentically to who we are, then what we had built wasn't authentic and if it died in the process of unbecoming what we were not, then it would be what it was. That sounds flippant and it wasn't. The work on myself was deeply intense, at times I saw the ugliest side of me and faced the darkest shadows.

I also saw the same in my husband. We are not perfect. We are people. We were people finding a new foundation, a new way of living, not just existing, a way of being honest and truthful and open, even at the cost of pain, at a cost of burning away what didn't work, what was built on the wrong foundation to find what did work and building a solid foundation.

And in the end, it worked, somehow, it worked. I guess underneath the masks, the anger, the frustration were expectations. I think we were both waiting for the other person to show up. I think we do that, especially in relationships, we wait. I don't want to be hurt by falling madly deeply in love with you so I'll hold myself back a little, one toe in with a whole foot out ready to run anytime.

I realized I was always ready to run and I couldn't build a healthy relationship if I was always looking for proof that he didn't love me, if

I was going to hang onto every little thing and store it, like poison in my heart to remind me not to let go too much. You can't be in and out at the same time. You can't protect your heart and be madly in love too. And without madly in love, what else is there? There is a safety. There is complacency. There is playing nice. There is "good" but that's not what I wanted, nor he was.

The more we moved through the phases and hung on, perhaps even him more so than I, because I was in the midst of trauma, deep exploration of my inner world, unpacking my stuff, and unpacking our relationship, while rebuilding a new business and a whole new me, he was there, always there. Anytime I got scared and wanted to run, I learned to lean in and every time I leaned in, he met me there, without words, just vibration and energy.

I can't say there was any one thing that worked for us to go from where we were to where we are except that we hung on and we gave the space for each other. We are independent by nature, not clingy, not needy and I think we because we are able to operate as our own persons outside of what makes us, us, that gave us the space. We didn't and don't try to be everything to each other.

And one day, like all the other storms, it was over. The frustrations melted into the background. It was just us, the real him and the real me. And we're people, we're not perfect and will never be, but somehow, we've grown through some hard times, deeply painful experiences, grown up together, grown closer together while still being individuals because we were willing to take off the masks, let down the walls and let the chips fall where they may.

No more damsel in distress, no more waiting for him, or anyone, to bust my walls down.

Now I enjoy being a woman in power because self-respect feels far more exciting and gratifying than feigned powerlessness to attract a weak man who can't handle a wild woman. Now my wildness is my power. And I bring out the warrior in my husband, not a man who needs to save me, nor one who needs to be placated or pacified, but a man who stands in the power of the divine feminine and hold it, in its chaos, it's mess, and enjoy it instead of dulling it.

He was home. The only home I'd ever really known. I spent my life running away from everyone and everything. I looked for proof that he couldn't be trusted. I focused on the wrong, the bad, the not good parts of him and us—all so I could run. Even though I wasn't leaving in reality, I was leaving constantly in my head.

My go to reaction to anything in life—leave inside. Put walls and barriers up. I'm not washing away the growth and the challenges we worked through. It was hard work for both of us. But I can recognize that when you're always running away, putting up walls and pushing people away, it's hard to address or deal with anything.

I guess that's what helped us. I stopped running. I stopped hiding. Instead I opened, I stayed and that for me was the hardest thing but it created a space, a deepening that allowed us to hold on when we had every reason to let go.

Rage is a step on the path. For in the rage and the willingness to burn it all down and see what remains is where we find ourselves, our tribe, who and what is meant for us.

There is a wildness to exploring that rage and instead of being burned by the fires that you set you are born of those fires. What didn't kill you, what didn't burn away, that's what real.

There is no pretending in that, no nice way to get that, no pleasing, lipstick wearing, perfection that can get there. It's a gutter move. It's a warrior fed up move. It's an over domesticated move. It's a suffocated soul move.

It's a wild woman coming move.

Through rage I exhausted myself. I pulled up the stories, the experiences, emptied the box. I spoke up. I yelled, screamed, kicked and cried.

And with each piece that I let go, I let go of the victim within. I cut the cords to the stories. When the anger was exhausted, I surrendered to the wild, my soul that was asking me to see with different eyes—my internal ones, the eyes of my soul—and it was there, exhausted, that I reclaimed my wildness.

I could finally save myself. I could finally use that sword that I had picked up so long ago.

I chose to live when I wanted to die. I chose to fight when I wanted to freeze. I chose to feel it when I wanted to run, I felt the fear and leapt anyway because nothing meant more than living, being alive, feeling alive.

To experience life, to live life is the best gift of all. We go through life giving up pieces of ourselves—we give them to people who take them, we give them to people who tell us to dull ourselves, change who we are and become something else.

We get conditioned, rewarded, punished, praised and chastised depending on our behavior. We let other people be right to keep the peace, stuff down our feelings, swallow our fear to fit in. We walk on egg shells and suffer in our own lives to keep other people happy and keep our place.

We get off our path to make someone else happy. Reclaiming ourselves means finding who we are in spite of all of that. Who am I? I am not simply what others want me to be. I don't have to be pleasing. I can fight back. I can be full of love and still have boundaries.

In fact, the most loving, authentic, happy people have healthy boundaries and know how to say no. They are not riddled with guilt and shame and changing who they are to make someone else happy.

While no one tells us this, it's the truth. I wasn't born to fit in. I was born to change the game, to change the rules, to stop fitting the mold and start building a new mold.

A wild woman knows her power, her strengths. She can see her flaws, her cracks, her weak places and she allows herself to be who she is. She is not afraid to explore her own darkness and she is not afraid of her light. When she is, she leaps anyway. Because she knows that the freedom she seeks is on the other side.

I am a warrior. And I can let my story be the proof others need to do their own healing knowing that it's simple but not easy. But that freedom from the chains that bind us, is on the other side of it.

We each have our own journey to finding ourselves, our own home within ourselves. My journey is different than yours but we'll be similar, we'll finally get to a place we knew existed but had never been.

That place is where we reclaim the lost parts of ourselves. The parts we lost to trauma, to conditioning and the parts we gave up as a trade for love, money, security.

If someone had told me 4 years ago that I would be here now, having the experiences I have, the people in my life I do and doing what I do I wouldn't have believed them. Sometimes we need to forget the big picture and show up each day knowing the big picture will take care of itself.

Sometimes we're not ready for that big picture just yet. The big picture is hidden under the baggage and we can't see the full expression of what's true, what's right for us, who we are, where we are going until we reclaim ourselves from own black hole.

Reclaiming ourselves is our right and privilege. Many people will never do that, never have permission, and never have the courage to do so. But for every woman who reclaims herself, she shines a beacon of light out there so other women can do the same.

Wild women are the future. The wild ones, the dreamers, the shakers, the lovers, the unconditioned, the untamed, the free spirit, the wild ones, the sacred witches, the ones who will forge ahead, who will die on the rocks, who will bleed out before they put the collar back on.

These women have come before us and will continue to come after us as the world continues to right itself from the hierarchy of ill-gotten power, as the paradigms are shifted, not to tear down men, but to rise up women and rise up the divine masculine within men.

The world is being righted as we are living in times of great collective pain. We cannot fight what we cannot see. The sexism, abuse, control, power, manipulation, racism, that has existed for centuries but was denied but is clearly on our door step now in a way that we cannot ignore it.

We do not have the luxury of ignorance and denial anymore.

The wild women are coming, born of the wild women who came before us. The ones who aren't conditioned, tamed or worried about being liked or good girls.

The ones who are setting fire, burning bridges, tearing down, walking away, screaming back. The ones who are showing up at the fire to bleed, to heal, to walk a new path back to themselves instead of who they thought they needed to be.

The time is now to do this work. We are at the shift of a new paradigm that many of us have been bringing in for a long time. We are in a revolution. The world is ready and needs a new way.

For every woman who stands up for herself, she stands up for others, and she gives others a space and the courage to stand up too.

Chapter Thirty-One

The last chapter to my life hasn't been written yet. In fact, I feel like my life is just beginning and I'm excited to see where it leads....

Epilogue

LET YOUR HEART BEAT WILD

It takes a lot of courage to do this. To find the broken, the hidden, the dark parts of ourselves and explore them. It takes courage to admit you need help, to know you cannot and don't need to do it alone, that vulnerability actually makes you stronger and more courageous and not weak like you fear.

It takes courage to look within, in a world that tells us to look outside and fix yourself—your money, your weight, your life with a product or diet pill or some magic wrap solution. It's not easy to decide to be you when that means you might lose people you love who no longer understand you.

Reclaiming our wild, breaking the chains that bind us to an unhappy life where we hide who we are is the point of this journey home…whatever you've experienced.

The reclaiming process starts with a decision to let yourself crack, to let the light in. Once that happens the journey will begin and the chapters will unfold. The chapters may not seem to make sense at times; only when the storm is over is it something that you can look back on and make sense of.

Let yourself breakdown, for the breakdown leads to the opportunity to build your life the way you want it. I remember thinking that if 'm not this, who am I? The body armor, the jaded, the anger, bitterness, frustration… if I'm not that who I am?

I didn't know. The rise helped me answer those questions—what do like, what do I want, who am I? The breakdown is unbecoming all that you are not so you can truly be who you are. You can't build a new life while holding onto the old one. You can't create a future where truly living life is the goal, if you are bringing the past into your present every chance you get.

There is a time for breaking down, letting go, releasing and there is a time for rebuilding. And each new phase of your life will require a different version of you. How that version emerges is to allow yourself to keep breaking down what is not you when it shows up, give yourself the space to release, to let go each time and in the place of what you release ask yourself what's your best next move? What would be the best thing to put in that place?

When you ask for something better, ask better questions, seek to find the truth instead of the pretty, know that because you asked, because you are operating from your own highest good that it will be filled with what you need.

Your journey is your own. The only thing you rob yourself of is the chance to truly live your life with your jadedness, bitterness and your sharp edges. I know. I lost far too many years holding onto, protecting, hiding out.

Sometimes it feels like the walls are safer but they are not. They become a prison of your own making. And holding onto the knife by the blade only poisons you, only poisons your life and robs you of the chance to live, not the person you're thinking or feeling about.

It's time to unshackle yourself, to let yourself be free of the fear, the stories and the old stuff that holds you back. It's time to reclaim you, to step fully into your own power and allow yourself the beauty and the gift of living life full out.

Throughout this process I opened myself to anything and everything. I wanted to experience, explore, see what vibed, what helped, what healed, what didn't. I experienced the traditional therapy route, and it didn't work for me. I felt so strange, sitting in those rooms with the stark light, the constant asking of the same questions and asking how it made me feel.

It was stiff, clinical and weird. The sand running through the hourglass and by the time I felt like opening up, it was time to go. Always. Maybe it wasn't my time. Maybe it was the space I was in. There are many amazing therapists out there, and I'm not knocking traditional therapy. It was part of my journey but were so many other things that seemed to get me out of my head and into my life through wild experiences filled with wisdom and metaphors.

I explored group therapy, regular therapy, and trauma therapies, in addition to the holistic work, shamans, sages, coaches, healers, mindset coaches, energy workers, retreats, events, and books. There is no one way. There's what works for you and be open to exploring because you could be like me, and find yourself in the unlikeliest of places because you were willing explore.

Explore the whole path, don't give up too easily or too soon, and be willing to branch off the path. Sometimes we have an idea of what path we should be on and we can ignore those side paths that take us in the most beautiful of places, to meet the most amazing people, and learn some big lessons, and end up back on our path, further ahead than if we had stayed pushing at the big boulder that was in the way of our own idea instead of going around it.

Life will give us boulders. Some we need to go around and some we need to go through and some we need to push out of the way with brute force. Some we need to sit on and take a rest.

Your own inner wild woman will lead you to the answer for each boulder that you encounter. I think our biggest problem as people is that we think we shouldn't have any problems so when we encounter challenges on our path we think it's not our path and we go home.

But the work was to find a solution and stay on the path. And sometimes that means being willing to explore, to take journeys, side roads to get armed with what you need to solve the problem in front of you.

Five years ago, I was a shell of a person who was living a duality—a real life where I pretended everything was fine and an existence of sorts where I slipped away so I didn't have to deal with anything.

My life wasn't enjoyable. I was going along with, I had no voice, I felt unseen, unimportant, used and walked on. I knew I wasn't happy and a series of life events caused me to wake up to how I had been living.

I had no idea that my journey would involve this work, these conversations and I wouldn't have started it if I had known that one day I'd be writing a book about the very things I wanted to bury forever.

It was only in my willingness to own my story, to write the chapters myself, to claim what happened to me as part of me, not a broken part but a part, like gold, that made me stronger because I survived it and could now talk about it.

Shame lives in silence. We cannot grow and change as a society if we are unwilling to look at suffering up close. It's easy to hate people from a distance, it's easy to see people's flaws and judge them.

I learned a lot of valuable lessons from this process and the number one lesson was that it's not about what happens to us but what we choose to do about it and who we become in the process of that.

Life will throw us curve balls, it will test us, beat us, burn us and tear us down if we let it. We cannot control it. We can choose to not live, to stuff it down, to hold back, and to not go after what we want. We can choose to believe those who told us we weren't enough.

We can choose to believe we are broken and damaged and not good enough when bad things happen to us. Or we can choose to rise. We can choose to heal, to feel it, to heal it, to reframe it and take the good from it and let the rest go.

We don't have to listen to the world. It doesn't mean you'll be the most popular. It does mean you will stir the pot, rock the boat and upend things. But if it comes to choosing between fitting in and living with purpose and passion and fulfilling your destiny, always choose to stand out.

When you weren't born to fit in, it can be a challenging world. It can be a challenging world to talk about the things we hide, our shame stories. It can be difficult to rise, to ask for help. It can be difficult to believe that you are good enough, that you are enough exactly as you are.

It can be difficult to love yourself when others tell you there's something wrong with you. It can be difficult to feel rejected and alone. And it can be very difficult to feel your feelings and explore your darkness.

But it's far more difficult to turn off who you, to turn away from yourself and your purpose and passion in order to be pleasing and fit in.

It's far more difficult to let the real you die and to become what you are not because you will always feel separate, broken, and as though you're hiding something. You will never live a life of peace and purpose, freedom and happiness, you will never be unchained as long as you hide who you are the things that made you that way.

That doesn't mean you have to tell everyone everything. Not everyone has earned the right to know your stories. Even in this book, I don't share all the details. Not everyone gets a front row seat, not everyone needs to and you don't have to care what they think about that.

Now is the time, wild one, to answer the call of your own wild soul, the wild woman inside of you that's clawing her way back to life. She has been beaten, burned and broken but when they buried you, they didn't realize you were a seed.

I have spent most of my life trading who I am for what other people wanted me to be, what they thought I should be. How have you been allowing someone else to dictate who you are?

When we allow ourselves to be who we are, our vibe will attract our tribe and that will bring us to people and places and things that are meant for us. That might not look like what you though it should. But it sure will feel like home when you get there.

In my life I have been unfairly persecuted and judged. And I have fallen in despair. Alone. I did these things alone. I have risen. Alone. I have clawed and crawled my way of the darkest holes, alone. And in me, it triggers old wounds, from generations of women who have also been persecuted, unfairly condemned, asked to be something other than they are, in exchange for love and acceptance, survival.

The wild within us wants to be free and when you have been born with that wild soul, that calling to step into something else, to rise we are going against the grain.

The world has set the stage for how it expects us to behave. And the bargaining chip is inclusion. But when your soul calls for something and those in your life require you to be something else to fit, choose your soul.

Because when you come from your soul you cannot go wrong. It might cost you a lot but what's meant for you will never be denied. Who's meant to be in your life will still be there after the bridges are burned and you rise from the ashes, the light from the fires illuminating your path forward.

I never make a wrong move when I come from my soul. When I feel connected, grounded and guided I know I am my most powerful.

When I move away from it, I feel an emptiness in my chest, a restlessness, a need to get away, run away, an anxiety, overwhelm and I make bad decisions from that space.

When I settle, hand on heart, drumming music vibrating through my body, clearing away the energy, the toxicity, the uncertainty, it all falls into place and I just know the answer.

Your box of darkness wasn't given to you by chance. It was given to you because you are the only one who can make sense of your box. You are the only one who can change the game for you and those in your vibe. They might not be the tribe you expected, they might not be the ones you even wanted, they might not be your family or your children or your lovers… your tribe, the ones who need your message, the ones who are waiting for you, need you to explore your own box of darkness.

Because in that box of darkness are parts of your soul, parts of your story that you need to bring back so you can fully live your own life—no more half living, no more living in shame, no more beating yourself up or lowering your standards or worth to fit in and be a part of something that you were never meant for.

When you let go you will find what is yours. And what is yours will be far better than anything you had to change yourself to get.

Being the wild woman is the biggest challenge I've ever faced. I've had to let go of my stories, stop playing the victim, I've had to rise when I wanted to fall. I've had to ask myself in the moments of self-sabotage who I need to be to get what I wanted? I had to ask myself how I was showing up.

What would the wild woman do?

I turned away from this book so many times because it seemed insane that I would publish something so private, so thorny, so prickly, so not perfect. But I would hear the wild inside scream *it's **not about you*** and I would listen for my heart beat, the beat of the wild, and I would settle into it.

Becoming unchained simply means letting go of all that we are not, all the ways we masked, we changed, we became what we thought we needed to be in order to survive.

Maybe you, like me, had everything that should make someone happy, but it didn't. Maybe you go to work every day, hating your life and wondering if this is all there is. Maybe you see, like my grandfather did, that life is about more than working and suffering and dying.

And it's not about letting people break our spirits. My spirit was broken over and over again. Each time I have been excited about something and shared it with someone who I thought would support me, be excited for me, only to hear him or her tear it apart.

Their voice becoming my own. Hearing their criticism on repeat until I eventually gave up my dreams. There will always be people who don't agree with our path, they will never see our dreams. I took it all so personally, not realizing that everyone sees through their own filter.

Some see the problems and some are scared of risk. Others are just too closed to new ideas. And others are jealous, triggered and want to tear apart people's dreams. And in the end, it doesn't matter.

And that had nothing to do with them and everything to do with me. If I was truly embodying the wild woman, what would I do, say? What if I uncensored myself?

What if I just let my heart beat wild?

What if I stopped expecting support and approval?

What if I stopped trading my voice and my wild for that support and approval?

What if I gave myself the permission, approval and validation I had spent so much time searching for?

Because giving up ourselves to get it, is trading. And that's not the wild, that's tame and my heart doesn't beat tame. My lungs don't expand properly when I'm tame.

I feel my best when I let the wild lead the way. I feel most me when I connect to my heart, listen to my soul, hear the beat of a drum and feel the bark of a tree.

When I feel the earth under my feet and feel the stars in my eyes, I know the wild is leading.

When I am judging and scared and closed and behind walls, when I am jealous and greedy and angry and keeping score. I am not wild. I am taming myself, I am caging myself, I am chaining myself. Because there I will be safe. There I won't have to step out and be brave. I won't have to put myself out there and risk being outcaste from humanity, left to be the biggest loser on the planet.

Those are the fears talking and listening to fear isn't the wild woman way. Listening to fear shows her the darkness and in exploring that darkness the wild woman finds more of her wild.

That is the process as I have uncovered it. Our shadow, our darkness is here to teach us, to help us remove generations of conditioning and condemnation of simply existing.

Women have been burnt, broken, beaten and enslaved for too long. We are here, now, at this time and this place, to awaken the wild woman, to let her rise, to let her out, she has been rumbling inside of you, of me, of she, for centuries.

When we heal ourselves, our own wild, we create the space for another woman to heal hers and we create the healing of the women who came before those—those endured immense suffering that caused us to live in fear and hide our wild for fear of the same fate.

It is time to rise up. It is time to throw off the chains, to stop listening to the world outside and start listening to your inner voice, your inner knower, to the wild woman that is inside of you.

She is the one who can lead you to freedom. And I know, wild one that is scary.

But you are strong enough now. You weren't once upon a time and you're scared it will consume you, that aren't strong enough to do this, but you are. Your wild woman will not break you, she will help you break down, she will help you feel and heal and then she will help you rise again.

For rise, you were born to do.

Let me promise you wild one, this won't actually break you, you think it will because the experiences will be soul shattering but it's not the soul that is shattering, it's the walls.

And behind those walls is your soul. Behind that identity, that persona you created to keep you safe. All you're doing is collecting all the pieces so you can feel whole again, here, in the now, in this life, living and loving as life was meant to be lived.

Life wants to love you. The universe has your back even when it seems like it doesn't. It will seem like it's here to break you wide open. And it is. And in that openness, you will not only heal your wounds but you will find parts of yourself you didn't realize existed because they have been gone so long.

And as you become who you really are, life will unfold in a way you couldn't imagine. And sister, it is beyond anything you've ever dreamed. It is far more magical, real and raw than anything your mortal mind can conjure up as a future.

You weren't born to sit on shelf and look pretty. You were born to be real, raw, authentic and open.

Don't underestimate your story or your part in this, wild one. For every one of us who rises we rise for ourselves, we rise for those who came before us and we rise for those who will come after us.

Burning it all down and rising from the ashes is necessary in order to be truly unchained. Unchain yourself from the prison you've lived, unchain yourself from the life of pretending and perfection.

Unchain yourself, wild one. The shackles have worn out their welcome, they are no longer needed. It is safe for you to rise, to be seen in all your power and for you to own all parts of yourself.

The world is anxiously awaiting your arrival.

You are wild. And as you stand wild, feet planted in the earth, you will feel the very heart beat of the earth vibrate through you and you will know, and feel that you are as wild as the animals that roam this planet.

There is always much to say on the topic of the wild. But in the end, the story is easy but the journey is not. When you are feeling dead, getting by, existing. When you feel your soul calling, that painful hole in your chest, your life, can't live another day like this, there has to be more than this to life—seize it—step into it.

Don't look away.

Allow yourself to stand in the storm, to unpack your box, to explore who you have been to others and what others have been to you. Allow yourself to sink, to remove all the parts of you that aren't real. Take off the masks. Stop pretending. Stop dulling and censoring and changing who you are.

Let what's not you be destroyed.

Reclaim the pieces of you that you find, the courage, the power, the fun, the excitement, the love—whatever is the gift in each piece of darkness—reclaim it. And reclaim you. Become who you always knew you could be.

I have trauma, I will be dealing with layers and levels of trauma my entire life. I will be challenged. I will have to overcome repeatedly. And it will when I'm not looking, when I'm not expecting it to be there, when something amazing happens.

And there's no shame in that. There is no timeline to get better or to get over it. It does lessen. The storm subsides and when something comes, it's easier to handle.

When you move from the wounded child to the empowered woman it's easier to spot the petulant child when she arrives. She's always here for a reason and listening to her, letting yourself feel and hear what she has to say will help you heal another layer.

Being wild isn't about being perfect. It's about letting yourself work through your process, being human, vulnerable, passionate, wild, bold, soft, speaking your truth and listening to your soul.

The dots always connect even when they don't seem to make sense. Trusting the guidance, listening to your soul, asking the next right move and taking the path even when you're scared, even when it doesn't make logical sense will lead you to yourself.

When you get home to you, the journey through the hardships, the pain and your purpose will blend together in a mishmash of truth, pain, vulnerability, excitement and humbleness of the power of the universe to bring you here in this time and this place to be who you are for what the world needs.

Life isn't easy. It has its ups and downs, it has its trauma's and mind-blowing experiences. How we stop participating in the continued hurt of the next generations, of each other, of the earth, animals is to do our own work—to take the journey through the dark night of the soul, to break down the walls and the barriers, to deconstruct the experiences and the beliefs that hold you prisoner to a life that is less than you can have.

Living authentically requires stepping outside the circle, standing on your own, being who you are in a world that is constantly telling you to be someone else, conditioning you to change, to blend in and fit in.

But you cannot live the life you were born to live, you cannot influence the world or help shift a new paradigm if you're too scared to be different, if you're too scared to open up, to be vulnerable, to let yourself break wide open.

My new life cost me my old one. And while many people tell you that all the things in your old life will be washed away, only the things that don't belong will be washed away.

My marriage is stronger. Because I stopped blaming and stopped pretending and instead of counting the ways he wasn't there or didn't support me, I counted the ways he did. And I spoke from my heart about who I was and what I wanted.

And in the end, it was just us, 2 souls longing for the love we already had but holding back because of life's conditioning and fear—fear of being all in, fear of being rejected, fear of being vulnerable.

All of my life is better because I'm real. My friendships are deeper. My goals are more aligned. I am more grounded, centered, empowered.

I cannot remember what it feels like to be the old me. I cannot imagine what it was like to know her. I cannot reconcile that were we ever the same person.

If I had been given a road map or told in advance the experience, I would have never taken the journey.

Because I love the woman I've become I cannot hate the experiences that brought me here. They are all part of the story of me and now I own them, they don't own me.

I am a strong, confident wild woman who is here to help others find and reclaim their power in life, to find their own inner warrior. I am la loba—the breather of souls. I help women take the same journey through their conditions and experiences and beliefs to their own wild soul. I never would have imagined I would be here. But as soon as I arrived I knew that all paths were leading me home to my own wild soul.

The same experience is available for you.

You do not need to set fire to yourself to warm another. You do not need to change yourself to fit. If you have to, it is not your tribe, they are not your people. Like the ugly duckling story, keep going until you find where you belong instead of changing yourself to fit where you don't belong.

Rise, wild one, rise. Your tribe is waiting for you to claim your rightful place.

We are waiting for you. Alone we are powerful but together we are unstoppable.

Let your heart beat wild.

WILD WOMAN MANIFESTO

Feel

You are a human being with feelings. Feelings are meant to be felt. Stop apologizing for feeling. Let yourself feel them. Shake with rage and anger and love and hurt. Let it pour out of you. And then it will be done. Don't store that stuff. It's not good for you.

Heal

Heal your wounds. No matter who created them. I promise you that healing might be painful but there will be nothing as painful as living life that was less than you deserved because you were too afraid to heal. Feel it to heal it and move through it.

Explore New Ideas

When you were young you believed because no one told you not to. Magic is available to those who believe. And it can help you on this journey into yourself. Ancient wisdom, shamanism, meditations, journeys can take you out of the ordinary into the extra ordinary, and that's where life begins.

Speak Your truth

Even if your voice shakes. Say you mean and mean what you say. Stand up for yourself. Defend others. The world needs more truth seekers and those who will stand up.

Rise

We do not have the luxury of choosing to remain silent. We are in the midst of a revolution. The divine feminine is rising. She is ready to come back and reclaim the world and through empowerment, kindness, and life. She is ready to use her sword and fight. She is ready to lay it down and listen. But rise, she will.

Take care of the mother.

Through the mother we came to be. The mother is the one who holds us and for us to even exist all that is supported by the mother. Take care of her in return. Spend time in nature. Don't support things and companies that destroy her. Help mother earth heal. And help the human mothers in your own life. They are struggling.

Let your heart beat wild

Hand heart. Go within. Ask. Know the answer will come to you in time. Your heart knows the way. Get out of your head and into your heart.

Listen to your intuition

That gut instinct, that deeper knowing? It's real. Listen to it.

WHAT'S NEXT?

The end of this book is the beginning of your journey. *Unchained* is a snippet of my own journey of unbecoming who I wasn't so I could be who I was born to be and my life's dedication and work is to help you become the wildest, best, truest version of yourself, too.

That's why I created some amazing tools for you to help you get started on your own journey of becoming—*UNCHAINED*.

Check out the amazing resources and get full access to what I've created for you by visiting www.wildsoulwomen.com/unchained.

9 781642 795561